SPORTS HEROES AND LEGENDS™

Jim Thorpe

Read all of the books in this exciting,
action-packed biography series!

Hank Aaron	Wayne Gretzky
Muhammad Ali	Derek Jeter
Lance Armstrong	Sandy Koufax
David Beckham	Michelle Kwan
Barry Bonds	Mickey Mantle
Roberto Clemente	Jesse Owens
Sasha Cohen	Alex Rodriguez
Joe DiMaggio	Wilma Rudolph
Tim Duncan	Annika Sorenstam
Dale Earnhardt Jr.	Ichiro Suzuki
Doug Flutie	Jim Thorpe
Lou Gehrig	Tiger Woods

Jim Thorpe

by Carrie Golus

TFCB Twenty-First Century Books/Minneapolis

Twenty-First Century Books
A division of Lerner Publishing Group, Inc.
241 First Avenue North
Minneapolis, MN 55401 U.S.A.

Website address: www.lernerbooks.com

Cover photograph:
© Bettmann/CORBIS

Library of Congress Cataloging-in-Publication Data

Golus, Carrie, 1969–
    Jim Thorpe / by Carrie Golus.
        p.   cm. — (Sports heroes and legends)
    Includes bibliographical references and index.
    ISBN 978–0–8225–7163–6 (lib. bdg. : alk. paper)
    1. Thorpe, Jim, 1887–1953. 2. Athletes—United States—Biography.
    I. Title.
    GV697.T5G65 2008
    796.092—dc22 [B]   2006101193

Manufactured in the United States of America
1 2 3 4 5 6 – JR – 13 12 11 10 09 08

Contents

Prologue
Nobody Is Going to Tackle Jim
1

Chapter One
Bright Path
4

Chapter Two
Carlisle
16

Chapter Three
Athletic Boy
26

Chapter Four
Summer Ball
37

Chapter Five
One-Man Team
44

Chapter Six
Olympic Hero
53

Chapter Seven
Athletic Marvel of the Age
60

Chapter Eight
Scandal
71

Chapter Nine
Baseball and Football
78

Chapter Ten
All-American
88

Epilogue
Glory Restored
95

Personal Statistics
98

Career Statistics
99

Sources
101

Bibliography
103

Websites
104

Index
105

Nobody Is Going to Tackle Jim

In Carlisle, Pennsylvania, in 1907, a young man named Jim Thorpe ran track at the Carlisle Indian School. Carlisle was a school for Native Americans.

Jim Thorpe was an exceptional all-around athlete. The high jump, long jump, hurdles, and mid-distance running events were all equally easy for him. But he didn't particularly enjoy track. He wanted to play football.

On the first day of varsity football practice, in September 1907, Thorpe asked an assistant coach for a football uniform. The coach replied, "Go away and come back when you have some meat on your bones. You're too light and too skinny. What do you want to do, get yourself killed?" When Thorpe insisted, the coach gave him a battered old uniform that was two sizes too large. Thorpe put on the uniform and trotted out onto the field.

1

Carlisle's head coach, Glenn Scobey "Pop" Warner, was furious when he noticed Thorpe. Football was an extremely rough game. At the time, school players wore no helmets or protective padding. Warner did not want his top track performer injured on the football field. But again, Thorpe insisted. Seeing how stubborn Thorpe was, Warner agreed to let him practice kicking, nothing more.

Kicking wasn't enough for Thorpe. Every day he asked Warner to let him join the rest of the players. Finally Warner decided to teach Thorpe a lesson. "All right!" Warner said. "Give the varsity some tackling practice!"

Forty Carlisle players spread out over the field, spacing themselves five yards apart. Thorpe, gripping the football, stood behind the goal line. Then he took off, racing past some tacklers, dodging others, knocking a few over.

Just over ten seconds later, Thorpe touched the ball down at the opposite end of the field. In his wake lay members of Carlisle's varsity team. Thorpe told Warner, "Nobody is going to tackle Jim!"

Warner stood staring, mouth open. Then he got even madder. He took another ball and slammed it into Thorpe's stomach. "Let's see you do it again," Warner said.

So Thorpe did. The second time, the run was harder, because the other players were determined to bring him down.

Nonetheless, Thorpe managed to fight his way through the defenders. He stood smiling in the end zone. Warner did not offer congratulations. Instead, he barked at an assistant to get Thorpe a uniform that actually fit.

Warner remembered years later, "After a lifetime of football coaching, I must admit that Jim's performance at practice that afternoon on the Carlisle varsity playing field was an exhibition of athletic talent that I had never before witnessed." Warner concluded, "Nor was I ever to again see anything similar which might compare to it."

Jim Thorpe's achievement that day was only the beginning. He went on to blow out the competition in not only football but also baseball and track and field. By the time he was done, the whole world recognized him as one of the greatest athletes who ever lived.

Chapter One

Bright Path

Stories about Jim Thorpe's family history vary and sometimes conflict. For instance, not all sources agree on his birth date. Most biographers think he was born on May 22, 1887.

Jim's full name was James Francis Thorpe. He and a twin brother, Charles (called Charlie), were born near modern-day Prague, Oklahoma. At the time, much of Oklahoma was named Indian Territory. The U.S. government had set aside the land as living space for Native Americans.

According to family legend, moments after Jim was born, his mother glanced out the window of the family cabin. She saw a streak of sunlight illuminating the path to the cabin door. From this sight, she gave Jim a Native American name, Wa-Tho-Huck, meaning Bright Path. (Many Native Americans at the time had two names—an English name used on official documents and a traditional Native American name.)

Jim's mother, Charlotte Vieux Thorpe, was of mixed French and Native American ancestry. According to one source, she was French, Potawatomi, Menominee, and Kickapoo. According to another source, her father was a wealthy merchant of French descent and her mother was Potawatomi. Jim's father, Hiram Thorpe, was also of mixed race. Hiram's father was of Irish or English descent. His mother was a full-blooded member of the Sauk and Fox tribe.

THE SAUK AND FOX

On his father's side, Jim Thorpe was descended from the Sauk and Fox tribe. The Sauk and Fox had originally been two different tribes from the Great Lakes region of North America. The two tribes were closely allied. Eventually, they came to be considered one tribe with a common language. In the 1800s, the U.S. government forced the tribe to move several times, because white settlers wanted their land for farming. By 1869 most of the Sauk and Fox had been resettled in Oklahoma, then known as Indian Territory.

Jim's parents had met around 1880, possibly at a powwow, a large Native American social gathering. Jim's father was known as one of the toughest men in Indian Territory. He was a top horseback rider, horse breeder, hunter, and wrestler. At one point, he worked as a whiskey trader.

With both Native American and European ancestry, Charlotte and Hiram honored some traditions from one culture and some from the other. For example, polygamy—the practice of having more than one wife—was common among the Sauk and Fox tribe. According to family legend, Hiram was already living with two wives and three children at the time he and Charlotte met. When he brought Charlotte back to their cabin, he told his first two wives that they could stay or they could leave. He didn't care one way or the other. The two women shared a wagon ride out.

But Charlotte was a devout Roman Catholic, a religion that forbids polygamy. After she and Hiram married, his polygamy ended. According to Thorpe family lore, they were first married in a Native American ceremony, then again at the nearby Catholic church. However, no official records of the marriage exist.

The couple had eleven children, including two sets of twins: Jim and Charlie and their older sisters Mary and Margaret, born in 1883. But life on the frontier was harsh, and only the toughest children survived. Six of the Thorpes' eleven children died in infancy or early childhood.

The family lived in a log farmhouse on about twelve hundred acres of land. The farm was on a reservation, an area set aside for Native Americans. Most of the other residents were

Sauk and Fox. The Thorpes' one-room cabin was dark, cramped, and crowded. But compared to their neighbors, most of whom lived in traditional bark shelters, the Thorpes lived well. The U.S. government agent who worked on the reservation reported that the Thorpe family was more "civilized" than most of the other residents. Unlike most of the tribe, the Thorpes wore European-style clothing rather than Native American clothing.

SECOND-CLASS STATUS

During the late 1800s, around the time of Jim Thorpe's birth, the U.S. government encouraged Native Americans to farm the land, learn English, and give up their traditional ways. But Native Americans were not even U.S. citizens. They did not have basic rights, such as the right to vote. In some cases, they were not allowed to leave their reservations. Native Americans were wards of the U.S. government. In other words, the government was in charge of them, the way a parent is in charge of a child. Most Native Americans did not get U.S. citizenship until 1924.

Jim grew up speaking English, because it was the only language his parents had in common. (Charlotte also spoke French and Potawatomi, while Hiram spoke Sauk and Fox.) Jim picked up enough of the Sauk and Fox language to communicate easily with others on the reservation. Unlike most of the Sauk and Fox tribe, both Charlotte and Hiram were literate. They had learned to read and write at schools for Native Americans. Although Hiram loved horses, he did not particularly enjoy farming. According to Native American custom, that job usually belonged to women. So Charlotte tended the family's fields of wheat, as well as the traditional native crops: corn, beans, squash, pumpkins, and melons. Hiram raised the family's pigs, cattle, and horses. "We always had plenty to eat at our house," Jim later said. This was an unusual situation in Indian Territory, where many people were desperately poor.

From earliest childhood, black-haired Jim and brown-haired Charlie were constant companions. They played on a rope swing that Hiram had hung over a river. They searched for wild blackberries, plums, and grapes. Hiram taught them to trap, fish, and hunt—sometimes with bows and arrows, sometimes with rifles. "Our lives were lived out in the open, winter and summer," Jim recalled. "We were never in the house when we could be out of it."

As a child, Jim Thorpe's favorite meal was fried squirrel with cream gravy and biscuits. It remained his favorite throughout his life.

In the summer of 1893, Hiram enrolled Jim and Charlie, then six, at the closest school—a school for Sauk and Fox children—twenty-three miles away. About sixty students, ranging from age five to age twenty, lived at the school. A religious group called the Quakers had founded the school to educate Native American children. The students attended classes and lived at the school for free. Jim's older brother George, as well as a half brother and half sister from Hiram's earlier marriages, were already enrolled there.

> Hiram Thorpe often organized wrestling matches and footraces at his farm. As a little boy, Jim enjoyed watching the men compete, especially when his father won—which he often did. When Jim grew older, he was allowed to compete too.

The Sauk and Fox school was in a clean, modern, three-story brick building. The school's white organizers had created the school not just to educate Native American students. They also wanted to stamp out Native American culture, which white people considered to be inferior. Students were forbidden to speak anything but English. They could not even speak their own native names. The school randomly assigned an English name to any student who did not have one.

Jim hated the school. The days were tightly structured, and the discipline was severe. Jim and Charlie had to march in step to their classes, where they learned basic reading, writing, and math. When they weren't in class, they did chores and learned job skills. Their life was a stark, unpleasant contrast to the free-wheeling childhood they had previously enjoyed.

Most of the other students hated the school too. One year, so many children ran away that the superintendent—the school's principal—asked for U.S. soldiers to help round them up. Among the runaways was Jim. His father, who was known throughout the reservation for his violent temper, beat him and returned him to school immediately. But Jim could be as ornery as his father. One teacher remembered Charlie as "a sweet gentle little boy," while Jim was "an incorrigible [badly behaved] youngster."

Jim's mother and father had a stormy relationship. Around the time Jim and Charlie went to school, their parents separated. During the separation, Hiram fathered a child with another woman. Hurt and angry, Charlotte filed for divorce. However, Hiram soon returned. By 1896 the couple was listed in a government document as "reunited under Indian custom."

While Jim never liked schoolwork, he began to enjoy some of the games students played at the Sauk and Fox school. He especially liked baseball, a new American game that was similar to the British game of cricket. Jim was a good all-around player: a fast runner, a hard hitter, and a fielder with a power-ful throwing arm.

> ❝When I was a kid, I didn't ever expect to get very far in sports. I wasn't big enough, for one thing. And the way we lived—[far] from everything—made it hard to learn. We didn't have a coach and most of the time we played barefoot. We made our own balls out of whatever was handy, used sticks for bats, flat rocks for bases, and made up our own rules.❞
>
> —JIM THORPE

In the winter of 1897, when Jim and Charlie had been at school for three and a half years, a typhoid epidemic hit the school. The superintendent and many of the students, including Charlie, were taken sick. Charlie also caught pneumonia. Hiram and Charlotte came to the school to help nurse their son, but it was no use. Charlie died. Alone for the first time in his life, Jim was devastated. His parents took him out of school that spring. He did not return until fall.

Without Charlie, school was even more miserable for Jim. The spring after Charlie's death, Jim ran away from school again. According to legend, when he arrived home, Hiram loaded him in a wagon and drove him the twenty-three miles back to school. Jim immediately escaped again, ran home by a shortcut, and met his father at the door of their cabin. While most people on the reservation were afraid of Hiram Thorpe, his eleven-year-old son was not.

The following fall, Hiram sent Jim to the Haskell Institute, another boarding (live-in) school for Native Americans. Haskell was three hundred miles away, in Lawrence, Kansas. It was far enough, Hiram hoped, that Jim could not run back home again. In many ways, Haskell was similar to the Sauk and Fox school. Haskell put the same emphasis on military-style discipline, basic education, job training, and the English language. But Haskell was much larger and more diverse. It had about five hundred students, ranging in age from five to the mid-twenties, from ninety different tribes.

The Sauk and Fox were famous for playing sports. In the early 1800s, autumn was time for the "great ball play." Games included lacrosse and a similar game called shinny. Sometimes, three hundred people or more played on each side.

Jim hated Haskell just as he had hated the Sauk and Fox school. The only bright spot was the school's strong sports program. At Haskell, Jim played football, another new American game, for the first time. Football had started thirty years before at colleges on the East Coast. Its popularity was beginning to spread nationwide.

Jim and other schoolboys often played with a makeshift ball—a stocking stuffed with rags or grass and tied at the open end. One day, the school's star varsity player, Chauncey Archiquette, noticed Jim playing ball and stopped to talk to him. Amazed at Jim's knowledge of football, Chauncey took Jim to a harness shop and made him a football out of scraps of leather. It was Jim's first chance to handle a real football—even though it was homemade.

In the summer of 1901, Hiram was seriously hurt in a hunting accident. When fourteen-year-old Jim heard the news, he decided to return home—no matter how far away it was. He jumped aboard a freight train, only to discover later that it was headed north, not south. So he got off the train and walked, occasionally hitching rides on farm wagons. Two weeks later, he had once again managed to run back home.

Hiram, by then recovered from his injuries, was furious that his son had defied him. But no matter how much Hiram beat him, Jim refused to go back to Haskell. Perhaps realizing he had finally met someone as hardheaded as he was, Hiram grudgingly let his son stay. Jim spent his days working on the farm, tending the cattle, hogs, and horses.

One afternoon, instead of doing chores, Jim and his older brother George went fishing. They knew they were risking a beating, and sure enough, they got one. This time, Jim had had enough of his father's abuse—he ran away from home. Just fifteen years old, Jim went to Texas, where he worked on a ranch, fixing fences and tending horses. "Of all my activities as a boy I liked best catching wild horses on the range," he later wrote. "At fifteen I had never met a wild one that I could not catch, saddle and ride. That is one achievement of my boyhood days that I do not hesitate to feel proud about."

Thorpe enjoyed his work but missed his family. Once he had saved up enough money for a team of horses, he decided to return. He arrived home to discover that his mother, age thirty-nine, had recently died from complications of childbirth. The baby, her eleventh child, had also died.

A few months afterward, in early 1902, Hiram married a white woman named Julia Mixon. The one-room cabin became more crowded. Jim lived there with his father, new stepmother, three younger siblings, and, soon, a baby half brother.

14

Hiram had still not given up on his hopes to educate Jim. A new public school, Garden Grove, had opened just a few miles from the Thorpe cabin. Hiram enrolled Jim there. Garden Grove was not a boarding school, which meant that students lived at home. And unlike Jim's previous schools, it was open to all students, not just Native Americans.

The teacher, who knew of Jim's reputation, asked him point-blank if he would run away from Garden Grove. Jim promised that this time—living at home, at a school that was not also trying to "civilize" him—he would not run away. To everyone's surprise, Jim kept his word.

Chapter | Two

Carlisle

In 1904 Jim Thorpe boarded a train bound for Carlisle, Pennsylvania. He was on his way to the Carlisle Indian Industrial School. Like the other Indian schools Thorpe had attended, Carlisle offered free tuition and free room and board.

It's unclear how Thorpe ended up at Carlisle. Walter White, his teacher at Garden Grove, claimed he told Thorpe that Carlisle was a good place for an athlete. Thorpe gave another explanation in a 1949 interview. He said a Carlisle administrator had traveled to Indian Territory in search of potential students. Thorpe asked about the possibility of studying electrical work, which he had previously studied at Haskell. The recruiter told him that Carlisle had no electrical program, but Thorpe decided to attend anyway.

Yet another explanation is in Thorpe's official file from the Sauk and Fox archives—historical documents kept by the tribe. The file contains a letter written to the Sauk and Fox agent and signed by Hiram Thorpe. In the letter, Hiram asks for help in finding a school for his son—a place where Jim could make something of himself, which he could not do on the reservation. But historians aren't sure if the letter is genuine. The writer of the letter gives Jim's age as nineteen—three years older than he was—and misspells both Hiram's first and last names, signing it "Hairm Thrope."

 Carlisle was the nation's first government-funded boarding school for Native Americans.

However it was that Jim Thorpe came to enroll at Carlisle, he arrived at the school in February 1904. With one thousand students, Carlisle was the largest school Thorpe had ever attended. At sixteen, Thorpe was older than a typical new student. Most students started around age twelve. Carlisle's oldest students were around twenty, although in special circumstances they were older. Like the others, Thorpe signed up for a five-year course of study.

Captain Richard Henry Pratt, an army officer, had founded Carlisle in 1879 in an abandoned U.S. Army compound. As a boarding school, Carlisle was designed to take Native American children away from the influences of their families and to educate them according to white standards. Pratt's motto was, "There is only one way: To civilize the Indian get him into civilization; to keep him civilized, let him stay." Carlisle teachers and students had to recite the motto along with him. The school usually had ten or so Sauk and Fox students. But Thorpe was assigned roommates from other tribes so they would have to communicate with each other in English.

PRATT'S VISION

Before becoming an educator, Richard Henry Pratt was a U.S. military leader. In fact, he was famous for fighting against Native Americans in the West. He led the Tenth Cavalry, the so-called buffalo soldiers. They were African American troops commanded by white officers. Pratt's experiences with black soldiers and Native American warriors led him to an unusual opinion for the time—that whites were not mentally superior to people of other races. Pratt believed that Native Americans could be the equals of whites if only they would adopt white culture. That idea led him to found the Carlisle Indian School.

On his first day at Carlisle, Thorpe and the other new students went to the barbershop. Just like soldiers in boot camp, they got short haircuts. Afterward, Thorpe and the other new students were issued military-style uniforms. During his time at Carlisle, he would be addressed as "Cadet Thorpe."

The schedule at Carlisle was similar to that of the other Indian schools Thorpe had attended. Half the day was taken up with classes, half with work. In the evening, students attended an organized study period. The school offered a liberal arts curriculum, similar to what college preparatory schools offered at the time. All Carlisle students studied music and art. In art class, they were not allowed to practice native crafts but instead produced European-style watercolors and oil paintings. At afternoon job training, male students studied carpentry, blacksmithing, tinsmithing, shoemaking, tailoring, or business. Female students learned domestic skills, such as dressmaking, cooking, nursing, and child care.

Like Haskell, Carlisle was noted for its sports teams, named the Carlisle Indians. Head coach Pop Warner and the other staff members respected the school's athletes, who were known as football boys or athletic boys, and gave them special treatment. But Carlisle's coaches initially overlooked Thorpe.

At sixteen, Thorpe was small for his age. In his school medical record, his height was listed as 5 foot 5. He weighed just 120 pounds. Chances seemed slim that he would ever land a spot on Carlisle's renowned varsity football team. But the school had various intramural teams (teams that played one another), based on the job skills students were learning. Thorpe, who was training to be a tailor, enjoyed playing with other students as a member of the tailor shop's football team.

Pop Warner

Glenn Scobey Warner earned the nickname "Pop" as a football player at Cornell University, where he was older than most of his teammates. After a short law career, Warner moved into coaching in 1895. He coached at several colleges before taking a job at Carlisle in 1899. In 1914 Warner left Carlisle to coach elsewhere. A youth football league was later named for him.

Pop Warner had a big influence on modern football. He was one of the first to realize that footballs travel farther and more accurately if thrown in a spiral. He also introduced padded uniforms and numbered jerseys and invented a number of important plays.

Not quite two months after Thorpe came to Carlisle, his father died. Different sources list different causes of death: blood poisoning, a hunting accident, and snakebite. Thorpe was deeply upset at the loss, especially since he received the news too late to attend his father's funeral. By seventeen, Thorpe had lost not only his twin brother but also both parents.

In June 1904, Thorpe was sent off campus on his first "outing." The outing program was the most famous aspect of the Carlisle educational system. Students lived in the homes of local white farmers for a work-study experience. While living among white people, Native American students were supposed to improve their English and learn more about white culture. Usually, these arrangements lasted for three months in the summer.

HIGH SCHOOL OR COLLEGE?

Carlisle's students ranged from middle school age (twelve) to college age (more than twenty). In some ways, the school combined elements of both a high school and a college. The superintendent once explained that Carlisle was a high school in the area of academics but a college in the area of athletics. Its athletic opponents were all colleges and universities.

Carlisle was not part of any athletic conference. Head coach Pop Warner scheduled games with whichever colleges or universities would agree to play. Only local teams ever played Carlisle at home. Otherwise, Carlisle always had to travel to play.

For his first outing, Thorpe traveled to Somerton, Pennsylvania, where he lived in the home of A. E. Buchholz.

Outing hosts were supposed to treat students like members of the family. But in fact, they often treated the students like low-cost employees. At the Buchholz home, Thorpe mopped floors, washed clothes, and peeled potatoes in exchange for just five dollars a month.

Thorpe had never spent much time working indoors. He hated the work and resented the low pay. He also resented having to eat in the kitchen with the rest of the hired help. Soon after arriving at the Buchholz home, he ran away from his placement and back to Carlisle.

There is no record of what happened to Thorpe once he returned. Discipline at Carlisle was strict, so he probably spent time in the school's guardhouse—a separate building similar to a jail. Nonetheless, Thorpe did not return to the Buchholz farm.

The following March, Thorpe went on a second outing, to the farm of James L. Cadwallader in Dolington, Pennsylvania. This time, Thorpe worked in the fields, which suited him much better. He stayed at the Cadwallader farm until July.

In September 1905, he went on a third outing, to the farm of Harby Rozarth in Robbinsville, New Jersey. Thorpe seemed to flourish there. He remained at the farm for a year and a half and was even promoted to foreman—supervisor of the other workers. In April 1907, Thorpe finally returned to Carlisle.

In 1907 Oklahoma became the forty-sixth state in the United States. In a ceremony at Carlisle, Thorpe marched with twenty-seven other Oklahoma students to celebrate.

But his life at Carlisle was about to change dramatically. According to legend, in the spring of 1907 Thorpe was walking across the track field on his way to play football with some friends. Members of the varsity track team were practicing the high jump. "I stopped to watch them as they went higher and higher," Thorpe wrote in his personal scrapbook. "After a while they had the bar set at 5 feet 9 inches and none of them could jump over it. They were just about ready to call it a day when I asked if I might try it."

Thorpe was wearing heavy overalls, a work shirt, and borrowed gym shoes. The other athletes snickered at him but agreed to let him try. Thorpe took a few practice sprints and kicks as he had seen the others do. Then, to the astonishment of the varsity athletes, he cleared the bar on his first attempt. Thorpe just laughed and went to join his football game.

Afterward, one of the high jumpers mentioned the incident to Coach Warner. Warner sent for Thorpe the next day. In his brusque way, Warner asked if Thorpe knew what he had done. At first, Thorpe thought he was going to be punished for breaking the rules by disrupting track practice.

INDIAN MASCOTS

Carlisle's athletic teams were called the Indians, making Carlisle the first team to use Native Americans as sports mascots. Later, many nonnative teams adopted Native American names, such as the Redskins, Braves, Chiefs, Savages, and Warriors, as well as names of specific tribes.

In the 1960s, Native American activists argued that Native American team names and mascots promoted offensive stereotypes. In 1970 the University of Oklahoma became the first school to drop its Native American mascot, Little Red. Since then, more than six hundred teams have followed suit. But several professional teams—the Atlanta Braves, Chicago Blackhawks, Cleveland Indians, and Washington Redskins—have kept their names, despite the controversy.

In fact, what Thorpe had broken was the school's high-jump record. "I told Pop I didn't think that [jump was] very high, that I thought I could do better in a track suit," Thorpe remembered. "Pop told me to go down to the clubhouse and exchange those overalls for a track outfit. I was on the track team now."

Over the years, the high-jump story has been told and retold. According to one version, Thorpe had never played sports before and was simply a natural athlete. But in fact, he was not a newcomer to organized athletics. Thorpe had competed for years in his father's informal track meets. He had played baseball and football at other schools he had attended. Yet for whatever reason, Thorpe had attended Carlisle for nearly three years without anyone noticing his standout athletic talent.

Chapter Three

Athletic Boy

In the spring of 1907, Jim Thorpe began training with the twenty-two-member Carlisle track team. Pop Warner asked the star of the team, Albert Exendine, to give Thorpe some intensive coaching to get him into shape quickly. Thorpe and Exendine became close friends—and remained so, even after Thorpe broke all of Exendine's records.

Thorpe was particularly good at the high jump, the long jump, hurdles, and mid-distance running events, although he liked other sports more than track and field. He wanted to play on Carlisle's baseball team. But baseball overlapped with the track season, and Warner wanted Thorpe on the track team. So Thorpe got to play baseball only at the very end of the season.

Thorpe's first college-level track meet was against Pennsylvania State College. He took second in the high jump, behind a Carlisle teammate. By the end of a strong season,

Thorpe had joined an exclusive club. He was considered one of Warner's athletic boys.

Athletes at Carlisle received special treatment. Thorpe moved into a more comfortable dormitory that was just for athletes. The athletic boys ate better food than the other students did and more of it. There would be no more outings for Thorpe because athletic boys were excused. Instead, Thorpe remained at Carlisle during the summers, doing light training and not much else.

All college athletes were supposed to be amateurs—that is, they could not receive any money for their athletic performances. The Amateur Athletic Union (AAU) and the National Collegiate Athletic Association (NCAA) enforced this rule. But Pop Warner (and many other coaches of the time) found creative ways to get around it. They quietly paid athletes in the form of travel allowances, clothing allowances, and expensive gifts.

After Jim Thorpe's astonishing tryout for the Carlisle football team in the fall of 1907—when he scored two touchdowns during tackling practice—Warner did not know what to think. Maybe Thorpe was the best ball carrier ever. Or maybe Carlisle's defense had some devastating weaknesses. Either way, Thorpe had earned a spot on the team as substitute halfback.

Once again, Warner relied on talented players to help Thorpe learn the basics of the game. Exendine had graduated but had returned to play football at Carlisle while preparing for law school. Exendine taught Thorpe how to block and tackle, while other members of the team taught him how to kick.

A SAFER GAME

Football has always been rough, but early football was an extremely violent game. According to one source, in 1905 eighteen college football players were killed during games and 159 were seriously injured. In 1906 the NCAA made substantial changes to football rules to make the game less brutal. The most important change was that forward passes longer than ten yards became legal. This rule change made the game safer, because players were less likely to get hurt moving the football through the air than by trying to ram it through a pile of opposing players.

Meanwhile, the entire team had to learn a new skill: how to throw the ball. In 1906, the year before Thorpe joined Carlisle's football squad, the NCAA had legalized the long forward pass. (The rules changed frequently in the early days of football. One year's game was often strikingly different from the last.)

Warner had opposed the rule change. But once the forward pass was legalized, he was one of the first coaches to take full advantage of it. Warner made Thorpe and the other players practice long passes—between thirty and fifty yards. To achieve such distance, Warner had his players throw the football in a spiral. (Before, players had just lobbed the ball at nearby teammates.)

Thorpe played his first football game against the Syracuse Orangemen in Buffalo, New York, on October 12. During the rough game, the starting halfback was injured. Thorpe went in as a substitute. He did not do anything impressive. He later admitted that he was so inexperienced that he barely knew the team's signals. Nonetheless, he played a solid game, helping the Indians win 14–6.

FOOTBALL AT CARLISLE—AMATEUR OR PROFESSIONAL?

Carlisle offered no athletic scholarships because students already received free tuition and free room and board. But Pop Warner often gave his players money in the form of expense payments or loans that were not expected to be repaid. Thorpe received a total of $500 during 1907 and 1908. This was a clear violation of amateur rules. In 1907 critics charged that Warner also paid his players for touchdowns, blocked kicks, and other crucial plays. Warner strongly denied the charges. But soon afterward, he stopped giving athletes cash. Instead, he gave them expensive gifts, such as watch fobs (decorative attachments for pocket watches).

A week later, Carlisle played Bucknell University at home. This time, Thorpe played most of the game as halfback. Late in the second half, he caught a kickoff and ran downfield. Just before he could score, he fumbled, but a teammate scooped up the ball and ran it in for a touchdown. The Indians won 15–0. Afterward, Carlisle's school newspaper wrote about Thorpe for the first time. It reported, "Thorpe did most of the work carrying the ball and proved to be an excellent ground gainer."

BIG MONEY IN SPORTS

In the days before professional football, the Carlisle Indians were one of the top attractions in U.S. sports. During the 1907 season, the team earned $50,000 from ticket sales, an enormous sum of money at the time. The money did not go directly to Carlisle but rather to the Carlisle Indian School Athletic Association, run by Pop Warner. The organization paid for all the athletics at Carlisle and Warner's large salary, which was much higher than the superintendent's. Leftover money went to build new buildings on campus, such as a hospital, a greenhouse, and an art studio.

On October 26, Carlisle played its biggest rival, the University of Pennsylvania. For Carlisle, the Penn game was the peak of the athletic and social season. Once again, Carlisle's starting halfback was hurt in the first half, and Thorpe took his place. The first time Thorpe got the ball, he lost yardage. The second time, he ran seventy-five yards to score a touchdown. The Indians beat Penn 26–6.

That year, 1907, was a magnificent one for Carlisle's football team. Of eleven games, the Indians lost just one, to the Princeton Tigers. The Indians defeated powerhouse teams from powerhouse universities, including Harvard and the University of Minnesota. They even beat the University of Chicago 18–4. At the time, Chicago was the undefeated champion of the Big Ten Conference. In most of the games, Thorpe did not play as much, or as well, as he would have liked. Years later, when asked about his first season, Thorpe replied, "I didn't like it much on the bench."

Next came track season. Thorpe was one of the team's strongest members. He was a tough competitor in the 120-yard hurdles, the 220-yard hurdles, the high jump, the shot put, the long jump, and the high hurdles. The team had other impressive members, including Frank Mount Pleasant and Louis Tewanima.

To Warner's frustration, Thorpe had talent but no real passion to excel. "He wanted to win, but that was enough," Albert Exendine said. "In races he sometimes took the last hurdle far in front [of the other runners] and then just strolled across the finish line." While Thorpe enjoyed beating the competition, he took no particular satisfaction in beating the clock. Thorpe did not enjoy training either. Nonetheless, he broke several school records in 1908.

When the track season ended, Thorpe played baseball, also coached by Pop Warner. By then the team was already nearly finished with its twenty-seven-game schedule. Before the season ended, Thorpe pitched a 1–0 shutout against Albright College.

That summer, the fourth Olympics of the modern era was scheduled for London, England. Thorpe competed in the high jump at the 1908 Olympic Trials but did not make the team. Two of his Carlisle teammates—Mount Pleasant and Tewanima—did make it. Thorpe spent the summer of 1908 in Oklahoma, visiting family members, fishing, and thoroughly enjoying himself.

In August 1908, Thorpe returned to Carlisle. At twenty-one, Thorpe stood 5 foot 11. He had filled out to 185 pounds. He had also developed new abilities in kicking the football and in breakaway running. Thorpe could punt a football so high in the air and run so fast that he could race down the field and catch his own punt.

The 1908 football season got off to a spectacular start for Thorpe. The first games were warm-ups, played at home against local teams. Carlisle played Conway Hall, the preparatory school for Dickinson College, on September 19. Thorpe ran for five touchdowns of fifty yards or more—all in the first half.

> ❝[Jim Thorpe] had a natural change of pace that just floated him past the defense. His reactions were so fast that sometimes you couldn't follow him with the eye. . . . He was fearless and he hit so hard that the other fellow got all the bruises.❞
>
> —POP WARNER

A week later, Carlisle and Villanova College were stuck in a scoreless tie. Thorpe was on the bench. With the crowd chanting, "We want Jim! We want Jim!" Warner finally sent him in. According to one eyewitness, "What followed was the single most dramatic play I have ever seen in sports." Thorpe crashed through Villanova's defensive line and ran seventy yards for a touchdown—without a single block. All he did was run, dodge, and holler, "Out of my way! Get out of my way!" The Villanova players obeyed. Warner immediately pulled Thorpe out, not wanting to risk an injury so early in the season.

The real season began when Carlisle played Penn State on October 3. The Indians were unable to score by running or passing, so Warner told them to focus on kicking field goals. (According to the football rules that year, field goals were worth four points, touchdowns five.) Carlisle won the game 12–5 because Thorpe kicked three field goals.

When Jim Thorpe was at Carlisle, footballs were the same length as modern footballs—between 11 and 11.25 inches—but slightly wider.

After defeating Syracuse 12–0, the Indians returned to Philadelphia to play the University of Pennsylvania. The Quakers scored first with a touchdown and an extra point. Then, in the second half, Thorpe ran sixty yards for a touchdown. With the extra point, the score was tied 6–6—and that is how the bitterly fought game ended.

Penn's team that year was in a league of its own. In fact, Thorpe's touchdown was the only one scored against Penn in its entire 1908 season. Thorpe later described the Penn game as the toughest game he ever played in more than twenty years of college and professional football.

Out of thirteen games in the 1908 season, the Indians tied one and lost just two—to Harvard and Minnesota. Thorpe's kicking ability that year won the attention of Walter Camp, a Yale coach often called the "father of American football." Beginning in 1889, Camp and a sportswriter friend, Caspar Whitney, selected the best football players in the country for their annual All-American team. After the 1908 season, Camp named Thorpe to the third-string All-American squad, mostly because of his impressive kicking.

SNEAKY PLAYS

Carlisle football players tended to be smaller than their competitors. So to win, Pop Warner and his team relied on running, field-goal kicking, and—after it was legalized—the forward pass. Warner also developed numerous trick plays for the Indians. He always made sure the plays stayed just within the rules. In one game against Harvard, a Carlisle player carried the ball by stuffing it up the back of his shirt. The so-called hunchback play did not win the game for Carlisle, but it became an infamous piece of football history. Warner used another trick in a game against the University of Chicago. A Carlisle receiver ran out of bounds, then back in bounds fifty yards downfield, where he caught a long pass to score a touchdown. Carlisle went on to win the game. Chicago's coach, Amos Alonzo Stagg, was still mad about his team's loss nearly fifty years later.

When the football season was over, Thorpe played basketball. And when the basketball season was over, it was time for track. In 1909 Thorpe was captain of Carlisle's track team.

Thorpe continued to excel at track, as he had the year before. At a meet in Syracuse, New York, in May 1909, Thorpe completely dominated the competition. He took first place in four events—the 120-yard hurdles, the 220-yard hurdles, the 16-pound shot put, and the long jump. He also took one second and two third places. "In the spring I tried him out in hurdling and jumping, and almost at once he became the star of the team," Warner recalled. "There seemed nothing he could not do."

Still, Thorpe was happy when the track season ended. Once again, he joined the baseball team as its schedule wound down. Before the season was over, he had pitched another 1–0 shutout, this one against Millersville State.

Thorpe preferred baseball to track for many reasons. For one thing, he thought baseball was a game with a future. At the time, baseball was the only established professional sport in the United States. The first professional league, the National League of Professional Base Ball Clubs, had been founded in 1875. Athletes could also play semiprofessional "summer ball" at numerous clubs around the nation. Track, on the other hand, was an amateur sport. Thorpe knew he would never be able to make a living by running and jumping. "He had his mind set on a professional career," Warner noted. "Many a time he moaned to me, 'What's the use of bothering with all this [track] stuff? There's nothing in it.'"

Chapter | Four

Summer Ball

As the 1908–1909 school year drew to a close, several of Thorpe's teammates decided to spend the summer playing semiprofessional, minor-league baseball. Summer ball was a popular seasonal job for college students and high schoolers with athletic talent.

Two of Thorpe's Carlisle teammates, Joe Libby and Jesse Youngdeer, had signed up with a new team, the Rocky Mount Railroaders, in North Carolina. Thorpe wanted to play summer ball too, so he tagged along on the trip south. The summer ball season had begun in May, about a month before Thorpe and the others arrived. Rocky Mount, which belonged to the Eastern Carolina League, was not doing well. The team definitely needed help.

Thorpe signed up with Rocky Mount for fifteen dollars a week. Officially, playing sports for money violated amateur regulations. A player who earned money for athletics could not return to the amateur ranks. Some summer ball players protected themselves from this rule by playing under false names. (According to legend, future army general and U.S. president Dwight D. Eisenhower competed in the minor leagues under the last name Wilson.) But Thorpe used his real name with Rocky Mount. Maybe he was too honest to lie or simply naive about the rules governing amateur athletics. Maybe he had no plans to return to amateur sports.

❝In 1909, we [Indian students] were having a rough time speaking English. We didn't know what the law was. We didn't know we were playing semipro ball. We didn't even call it that. We called it summer ball.❞

—CARLISLE STUDENT JOE LIBBY

In any event, Thorpe started with Rocky Mount at third base. "After a while, the manager asked me if I could pitch," Thorpe wrote later in his personal scrapbook. He pitched a number of games for the team that year.

Thorpe played his first semiprofessional game against the Raleigh Red Birds. He struck out his first two times at bat, and the Railroaders lost 5–1. The next day, Thorpe pitched. He allowed just five hits while getting two hits himself.

By the season's end, Thorpe had played in forty-four games as a pitcher and infielder. His batting average was .253—about one hit for every four at bats, or 25 percent. The most impressive thing about Thorpe was not his throwing or hitting but his speed. If Thorpe hit a ground ball, there was almost no point in fielding it, because he was already safe on first base.

BATTING AVERAGE

A batting average is the number of times a player gets a hit compared to the number of times at bat. For example, an average of .200—20 percent—means the player got one hit for every five at bats. In modern professional baseball, a batting average of .300 or better is considered good. Less than .250 is poor, and less than .200 is unacceptable. Batting .400 or higher for a season is thought to be nearly impossible. No one has managed it since 1941.

Summer ball in the Eastern Carolina League was informal, even chaotic. Players often left for other teams in the middle of the season. By August, Thorpe was the only Carlisle player left on the Rocky Mount team. Teams argued over balls that were supposedly tampered with and games that were supposedly fixed. Even worse, at the end of the season, three of the six teams in the Eastern Carolina League claimed they had won the league championship. Finally, the league president resigned, calling his own league a "laughingstock."

Thorpe's personal life was chaotic too. At twenty-two, he had lived most of his life in restrictive boarding schools. At Carlisle, Pop Warner and the other coaches had made sure he stayed out of trouble. In North Carolina, Thorpe was free to do as he pleased for the first time in his life. He did not handle his new freedom well. He often drank too much and got into fights.

One night Thorpe was arrested for fighting in a bar in Raleigh. He resisted arrest and ended up spending the night in jail. Another night Thorpe dumped a police officer upside down into a garbage can. Four more officers worked together to finally subdue him. The incidents did not hurt Thorpe's baseball career. He paid fines as punishment and kept on playing ball.

When the season ended in September, Thorpe decided not to return to Carlisle. Instead, he traveled back to Oklahoma, where he worked on his sister Mary's farm in exchange for room and board.

Without Thorpe, Carlisle's football team was noticeably weaker. The Indians lost to Penn and Brown and lost to Pittsburgh for the first time ever. At Thanksgiving, Thorpe traveled to Saint Louis, Missouri, to see his old team play Saint

Louis University. It was the final game of the season and one of the Indians' best. They won 32–0.

After the victory, the team returned to school, but Pop Warner stayed behind to spend some time with Thorpe. The two took a hunting trip in eastern Oklahoma. There, Warner asked Thorpe to return to Carlisle. Thorpe did visit Carlisle at Christmas. He promised that he would return in the spring for track season and football training. But for whatever reason, he did not keep his promise. Instead, he traveled back to North Carolina to play with the Railroaders that spring. Thorpe hurt his arm early in the season. When he recovered, he batted .236 in twenty-nine games.

Pop Warner was annoyed that he lost so many promising athletes to semiprofessional baseball. In 1910 he persuaded Carlisle's new superintendent, Moses Friedman, to drop baseball as a varsity sport so that Carlisle would no longer be a training ground for semipro ballplayers. In its place Warner added lacrosse, a traditional Native American sport.

Thorpe's strength remained his baserunning. Sometimes he amused the crowd by showing off his track-and-field skills.

In one game, Thorpe was already on base when a teammate hit a single to right field. Thorpe took off running for home. Twenty-five feet away, he let out a yell and long-jumped onto home plate, to the delight of the crowd.

On August 12, Thorpe was traded to the Fayetteville Highlanders. He played with them for sixteen games and batted .250. Near the end of the season, Thorpe was hit in the head with a ball while trying to steal second base. As blood gushed from the wound, the crowd gasped. But Thorpe just laughed. He spent the end of his second minor-league season in the hospital recovering.

Thorpe spent another fall, winter, and spring working for relatives in Oklahoma. In the summer of 1911, he played his third year of summer ball. That season, he stayed near home, playing for a team in Anadarko, Oklahoma. The team did not belong to a formal league, and at the beginning of the season it did not even have a name. Nonetheless, it was good.

By the end of July, the Anadarko Champions—as the team was by then called—had won thirteen straight games. More than one thousand spectators came to see Thorpe and the others play against teams from Oklahoma City and Chicago. The Champions ended the season with forty-five wins and four losses.

One day that summer, Thorpe ran into Albert Exendine, his old friend, coach, and teammate. Exendine, who had grown up in Anadarko, was back in his hometown for a visit. By then he had earned a law degree and was coaching at a small college. When Thorpe said he hadn't been up to much, Exendine suggested that he finish his degree at Carlisle.

Thorpe was worried that Carlisle would not want him back, and he was right. Superintendent Moses Friedman was not impressed with Thorpe as a student and did not want him to return. But Pop Warner desperately needed Thorpe. Carlisle's 1910 football season, with eight wins and six losses, had been the worst for years. Warner convinced Friedman to let Thorpe back into school.

According to Thorpe, when he arrived back at Carlisle in September 1911, Warner asked him where he had been. Thorpe told him honestly that he had been playing baseball. Later on, Thorpe enjoyed telling the other athletic boys stories about his years playing semipro ball—even when coaches were listening nearby. "I never made any secret about it," Thorpe later recalled.

According to NCAA and AAU rules, a player such as Thorpe, who had earned money in sports, should not have been allowed to return to the college ranks. Yet the coaches welcomed Thorpe back at Carlisle.

Chapter Five

One-Man Team

With Jim Thorpe back, the 1911 Carlisle Indians football team could not have been more different than the previous year's mediocre team. As usual, the season began with warm-up games, played at home against local colleges. Carlisle beat Lebanon Valley College 53–0, Muhlenberg College 32–0, and Dickinson College 17–0. In the Dickinson game, Thorpe made an impressive eighty-five-yard run to score a touchdown.

In the final warm-up game, against Mount Saint Mary's College, Thorpe scored three touchdowns in the first half. Mount Saint Mary's was the first opponent of 1911 to score against the Indians. Still, the final score was 46–5.

These opponents were not as well funded and well trained as the top college teams Carlisle played later in the season. But the Dickinson team impressed Warner. He asked it to scrimmage (practice) with Carlisle every Wednesday for the rest of the season.

Carlisle's first away game was against Georgetown in Washington, D.C. Thorpe did not score any touchdowns. But his kicking, running, and tackling made key contributions to Carlisle's 28–5 victory.

---

66 *When you're talking about Big Jim's football ability you can't exaggerate. He was just the greatest, that's all.* 99

—Vic "Choc" Kelley, a Carlisle teammate

On October 21, Carlisle played the University of Pittsburgh. Twice, Thorpe managed to run downfield and catch his own punt. After one of these catches, he scored a touchdown. A reporter for the *Pittsburgh Dispatch* described Thorpe as "tall and sinewy, as quick as a flash and as powerful as a turbine engine. . . . Kicking from fifty to seventy yards every time his shoe crashed against the ball, he seemed possessed of superhuman speed."

The next week the Indians played Lafayette College in Easton, Pennsylvania. Thorpe scored a touchdown and extra point and kicked a thirty-five-yard field goal. The final score was 19–0. But Thorpe also severely twisted his ankle during the game. Carlisle's top rival, the University of Pennsylvania, was scheduled for the next week.

Thorpe tried to run and kick before the Penn game, but he was in too much pain. To his frustration, he ended up sitting on the bench. Nonetheless, the team rallied and was able to win 16–0.

For Thorpe, the Philadelphia trip had one bright spot. A closely chaperoned group of female students was traveling along with the team. After the game, the players and their dates had dinner together in the city. Thorpe's date was Iva Miller, a Carlisle girl he had danced with at Saturday socials. Miller was one of the brightest, prettiest students in the senior class.

The next week, Carlisle was scheduled to play Harvard. All week long, Warner worked on Thorpe's injured ankle. He tried to speed its healing with massage, liniment, vibrating machines, even jolts of electricity.

On the day of the game, November 11, 1911, more than forty thousand fans packed Harvard Stadium, then the nation's largest college sporting arena. Harvard had fifty players on its team, compared with Carlisle's sixteen. Harvard's head coach was so sure of his team's superiority that he told his assistant coaches to use the second-string team. He wanted to save his starting team for important upcoming games against Dartmouth and Yale.

Thorpe's ankle was still giving him trouble. So Warner encased the ankle in plaster to help protect it and sent Thorpe out on the field. At first Thorpe was stiff and unsteady. But despite his injury, he kicked two field goals in the first half and a third in the second half. He even forgot his injured ankle and started running the ball, gaining 173 yards in the second half.

By the fourth quarter, the Indians were ahead 15–9. In desperation, the Harvard team captain decided to disregard the head coach's orders. He led the first-string team onto the field. Harvard managed to score a touchdown in the final few minutes, but Carlisle was already too far ahead. The final score was 18–15.

At the very end, Thorpe's ankle gave way. Unable to walk, he had to be carried off the field by his teammates. Even the Harvard fans cheered. Afterward, the Harvard coach said about Thorpe, "I realized that here was the theoretical superplayer in flesh and blood."

Thorpe, Warner, and the rest of the team had hoped for an undefeated season. But their hopes were crushed the very next week in a game against Syracuse. Thorpe scored both of Carlisle's touchdowns in the game, including one in the last two minutes. But his effort was not enough—Syracuse won 12–11. Thorpe was bitterly disappointed. Despite his impressive scoring, he blamed himself for missing the kick that would have earned an extra point and tied the game.

Two more victories followed, over Johns Hopkins and Brown. In the Brown game, the final one of the season, Thorpe impressed the crowd with an eighty-three-yard punt. Carlisle won 12–6. On the train back to Carlisle, Thorpe was elected captain of the 1912 squad. Later, Walter Camp named Thorpe a first-team All-American halfback.

With football season over, Thorpe joined Carlisle's basketball team. He dropped basketball when the track season started. Meanwhile, Thorpe's friendship with Iva Miller, the pretty and popular honors student, was becoming more serious. Miller, from Pryor Creek, Oklahoma, was a nursing student. In 1911 she was eighteen years old, six years younger than Jim Thorpe. Unusual for a Carlisle student, Miller had only a trace of Native American blood.

Miller graduated in April 1912. Thorpe was also a member of the class of 1912, but he did not graduate. Despite his years of schooling at Carlisle, he had not earned enough credits for a certificate.

A Poet at Carlisle

During his final terms at Carlisle, Thorpe studied business. One of his teachers was Marianne Moore. She taught math, typing, and law. Moore was fond of Thorpe, although he often missed class. When he did attend, he was usually unprepared. At Carlisle, Moore was an aspiring poet. She later won the Pulitzer Prize and the National Book Award for her modernist poetry.

For Thorpe, his academic standing was much less important than his next goal: the 1912 Olympic Games, to be held in Stockholm, Sweden. During the winter of 1912, Pop Warner took Thorpe and Louis Tewanima to as many indoor track meets as possible. In February, at a Boston Athletic Association meet, Thorpe broke the Carlisle high-jump record with a leap of 6 feet, 0.5 inch. In March, at the Pittsburgh Athletic Club Indoor Meet, Thorpe won four of the five events he entered: the 60-yard dash, the 60-yard hurdles, the 12-pound shot put, and the high jump. It seemed certain that Thorpe would qualify for the Olympic track team.

On May 18, 1912, Thorpe traveled to New York for the Olympic Trials. "Jimmy Thorpe, the wonderful Carlisle athlete, proved to be in a class by himself," the *New York Times* reported afterward. Thorpe made the Olympic team in two events—the pentathlon and the decathlon.

❝ *The first event I saw him in was the shotput. He did everything wrong: his stance, his footwork, his follow-through. It was all backwards. Warner never taught him a thing. He probably just handed him the shot, and said, 'Here, throw this.' But Thorpe beat every shot-putter in the [Olympic] trials.* ❞

—ABEL KIVIAT, ONE OF THORPE'S OLYMPIC TEAMMATES

The pentathlon was a new Olympic event. It was based on an ancient Olympic competition. The pentathlon included five separate competitions: the long jump, the javelin throw, the 200-meter dash, the discus throw, and the 1,500-meter run. The decathlon, devised by the Swedes, was even more challenging. It included ten competitions: the 100-meter race, the long jump, the shot put, the high jump, the 400-meter race, the 110-meter the high hurdles, the discus, the pole vault, the javelin, and the 1,500-meter race.

Both the pentathlon and the decathlon were designed to test an athlete's all-around ability. In both contests, competitors received a point score for each event. At the end of the competition, the athlete with the highest score was the winner.

The words *pentathlon* and *decathlon* are of Greek origin. *Penta* means "five," and *deca* means "ten." *Athlon* means "contest."

At the end of May, Carlisle had its final track meet, against Lafayette College in Easton, Pennsylvania. Carlisle had just seven athletes, competing against more than thirty from Lafayette. Yet Carlisle won the meet easily—a typical victory.

In mid-June, Thorpe and Tewanima left Carlisle to prepare for the Olympics. They traveled to Pop Warner's home in Springville, New York. For several weeks, the two athletes lived with Warner and trained at a local athletic field.

At the time, the modern Olympics was still a fairly new phenomenon. Athletes were poorly funded. The U.S. Olympic Committee raised more than $100,000—an extraordinarily large sum in 1912—to help cover the expenses of the athletes. Still, Thorpe and the other athletes had to pay some of their own way.

As a Native American, Thorpe had two sources of income. He owned land in Oklahoma—the result of various treaties his tribe had signed with the U.S. government. He rented the land to a farmer. He also received an annuity, a regular payment from the U.S. government. But Thorpe did not have free access to his own money. The government agent for the Sauk and Fox tribe controlled all tribe members' money. In May 1912, Thorpe wrote to the Sauk and Fox agent, asking for $100 from his account. Carlisle's superintendent, Moses Friedman, seconded the request.

As often happened, the agent refused. In a letter to Friedman, the agent wrote, "[Thorpe] has now reached the age when, instead of gallivanting around the country, he should be at work on his allotment [his Oklahoma land]." If Friedman and

Warner had not given Thorpe some money at the last minute, he never would have made it to Stockholm for the 1912 Games. "Unfortunately, amateur athletics is not for the poor and friendless," Warner later observed.

Chapter Six

Olympic Hero

On June 14, 1912, Jim Thorpe, Louis Tewanima, Pop Warner, and the other Olympic athletes boarded a ship, the SS *Finland*, bound for Europe. The journey across the Atlantic Ocean took ten days. Thorpe said later that boarding and touring the immense ship was the biggest thrill of the Olympic trip.

During the voyage, the 168 U.S. athletes trained as hard as possible, within the limits of the ship. Track-and-field athletes made do with a 100-yard cork track. Swimmers had to practice in a small canvas swimming pool. They swam in place, tied to the edge of the pool with ropes. Thorpe ran laps, lifted weights, and did calisthenics daily along with the other Olympians.

The ship docked first in Antwerp, Belgium, for a few days, then continued on to Stockholm. The city had no Olympic

Village to house athletes (the first Olympic Village was built in Los Angeles for the 1932 Summer Olympics). In Stockholm, the U.S. team used the *Finland* as its headquarters.

The opening ceremonies were held on July 6, 1912. Twenty-five-year-old Jim Thorpe was among the twenty-five hundred athletes from twenty-seven countries who marched into the newly built Olympic stadium. The next day, the pentathlon began. It was the first-ever international competition in the event, which previously had been held only in Europe. Because of that experience, Europeans were expected to dominate the competition.

But expectations changed when Jim Thorpe began to compete. The first event was the long jump. Thorpe hit the takeoff mark perfectly and sailed through the air. With a leap of 23 feet, 2.7 inches, he took first place. Thorpe's weakest event was the javelin. With a throw of 153 feet, 2.95 inches, he took second. He won first place in the next two events, running the 200 meters in 22.9 seconds and throwing the discus 116 feet, 8.4 inches.

The final event was the 1,500-meter run. A U.S. teammate and a Norwegian set the pace for the first lap. But halfway through the second lap, Thorpe took over. He passed both leaders to finish the race in 4 minutes, 44.8 seconds. With wins in four of the pentathlon's five events, Thorpe easily took the gold medal. "His all-around work was certainly sensational," James Sullivan of the AAU said after Thorpe's pentathlon victory. Sullivan also said that "Thorpe is a real American if there ever was one."

The decathlon wouldn't start for another six days. Rather than resting up for his next demanding competition, Thorpe decided to informally enter individual track-and-field events. He told a coach that he wanted to enter as many events as he could. "What's the fun in watching someone else?" he said.

Thorpe did not excel in the individual events, which were dominated by real specialists. In the high jump, he tied for fourth place. In the long jump, he took seventh. But spectators were amazed that Thorpe could go from one strenuous event to another without tiring.

 In 1912 Olympic events were wide ranging. They included everything from shooting deer to a writing contest.

The decathlon was scheduled for the final three days of the Olympics. Thorpe would be competing against an elite group of twenty-eight talented, all-around athletes.

On July 13, the first day of the decathlon, it was pouring rain. It was a bad sign for Thorpe, who did not do his best, in either track or football, during bad weather. Three events—the 100-meter dash, the long jump, and the shot put—were scheduled that day.

Thorpe ran the 100-meter dash, which he normally did in less than 10 seconds, in 11.2 seconds. That time put him in second place in the event, behind a U.S. teammate. He had even more trouble in the long jump. The takeoff board was wet and slippery. Twice, Thorpe committed a fault by stepping over the line where he was supposed to begin his jump. He had only three chances.

But Thorpe looked calm as he walked up for his third try. This time, he ran carefully down the track, hit the mark, and jumped 22 feet, 2.3 inches. That jump put him in second place for the event. More important, it kept him in the running for the overall competition. In the final event of the day, the shot put, Thorpe also came in second. Although he had not won a single event, his point total gave him a slight lead over the other competitors.

The next day the rain stopped, and Thorpe's performances improved. He won the high jump with a leap of 6 feet, 1.6 inches. In the 400-meter run, he came in second with a time of 52.2 seconds. He also placed second in the discus throw. Thorpe won the day's last event, the 110-meter hurdles, in 15.6 seconds.

The final day of the decathlon included two events that were not Thorpe's strongest, the pole vault and the javelin throw. In the pole vault, he placed third. In the javelin, he came in fourth—his lowest ranking of the competition. The final event of both the decathlon and the Olympics was the 1,500-meter run. Thorpe ran it in 4 minutes, 40.1 seconds, beating his own winning time in the pentathlon.

When the points were tallied using a complicated formula, Thorpe had won a second gold medal. He ended up far ahead of the second-place competitor, Hugo Wieslander of Sweden. "At no time during the competition was I worried or nervous," Thorpe later wrote in his scrapbook. "I had trained well and hard and had confidence in my ability. I felt that I would win."

Jim Thorpe is the only athlete in Olympic history to win both the pentathlon and decathlon. The pentathlon was discontinued after the 1924 Olympics, which meant that athletes no longer had a chance to match Thorpe's achievement.

The awards ceremony for the entire Olympics was held later that afternoon. U.S. athletes received sixteen gold medals—two of them won by Jim Thorpe. Sweden's king, Gustav V, presented the medals to the athletes. When Thorpe approached the podium to accept the gold medal for the pentathlon, a mighty cheer rose from the crowd.

As well as gold medals, Jim Thorpe got two prizes for his Olympic victories. For winning the pentathlon, he received a life-size bronze bust of the king of Sweden. For his victory in the decathlon, he got a chalice—a large ceremonial cup—in the form of a Viking ship (the Vikings were fierce Scandinavian warriors). The chalice, which weighed thirty pounds and was covered in gold and semiprecious stones, was a present from Czar Nicholas II, the emperor of Russia.

Jim Thorpe grew up speaking English and wearing European-style clothing. However, he preferred outdoor work and play to studying in school.

Thorpe poses in his Carlisle Indian School football uniform around 1909. Players wore very little protective clothing during the early years of football.

Thorpe threw the discus in the pentathalon at the 1912 Olympic Games in Stockholm, Sweden. The other events in the pentathalon were the 200-meter dash, the long jump, the javelin throw, and the 1,500-meter race.

Louis Tewanima *(left)*, Pop Warner *(center)*, and Thorpe *(right)* traveled to the 1912 Olympic Games together. Tewanima was another member of Carlisle's track team. Warner coached Carlisle's football, baseball, and track teams.

King Gustav of Sweden *(right, on stage)* congratulated Thorpe *(left, holding hat)* on his Olympic triumphs. Thorpe, wearing the laurel wreath given to all gold-medal winners, was awarded the life-size bust next to the king.

Thorpe poses during training camp with the New York Giants. He played baseball for the Giants between 1913 and 1918.

Thorpe played for several different professional football teams over the years. He was known for his ability to punt the ball so long and high that he could run downfield and catch his own kick.

Thorpe married Freeda Kirkpatrick in 1925. The couple settled in Ingleside, California, and had four sons.

Thorpe *(center)* sometimes wore traditional Native American garments at speaking engagements and other appearances. In this 1932 photo, he joins members of eighteen Native American groups to demonstrate for the rights of Native American actors in the motion picture industry.

Six of Jim Thorpe's children surround International Olympic Committee president Juan Antonio Samaranch *(center)*. This ceremony to reinstate Thorpe's two Olympic gold medals took place on January 18, 1983. Jim Thorpe had been dead for almost thirty years.

The cheer was even louder when Thorpe received the final award of the ceremony, the gold medal for the decathlon. After making his presentation, the king shook Thorpe's hand and said, "Sir, you are the greatest athlete in the world." In his scrapbook, Thorpe described that moment as the proudest of his life.

Chapter Seven

Athletic Marvel
of the Age

After the Olympics, Jim Thorpe and a few other U.S. athletes remained in Europe to compete in a series of post-Olympic meets. In Reims, France, Thorpe ran the 100-meter high hurdles in 15.6 seconds, beating the Olympic gold medalist. But at another meet, in Paris, France, Thorpe lost in the hurdles because an airplane flew over the stadium. Airplanes had been invented less than a decade earlier, and Thorpe had never seen one before. When he heard the plane, he looked up, his foot hit the hurdle, and he fell facedown on the cinder track. Thorpe didn't care about the loss, one teammate recalled. He was too excited about seeing his first plane.

On August 16, 1912, Jim Thorpe, Louis Tewanima, and Pop Warner returned to Carlisle. A cheering crowd gathered to greet them. The city had officially declared August 16 to be "Thorpe Day." Every business in town was closed. Celebrations included a parade, a track meet, a baseball game, a formal reception at Carlisle, a band concert, and fireworks.

"By your achievement you have immeasurably helped your own race," Carlisle superintendent Moses Friedman told Thorpe during a speech. "By your victory you have inspired your people to live a cleaner, healthier, more vigorous life."

Friedman also read aloud a congratulatory letter to Thorpe from U.S. president William Howard Taft. "You have set a high standard of physical development which is only attained by right living and right thinking," Taft wrote, "and your victory will serve as an incentive to all to improve those qualities which characterize the best type of American citizen." (Ironically, as a Native American, Thorpe was not a U.S. citizen at the time.)

On August 24, Thorpe, Tewanima, and Warner joined other Olympic medalists for a victory parade down Fifth Avenue in New York City. Each athlete sat in a car, with his name marked on the front. A crowd of almost one million people came out to see the Olympic champions.

Thorpe was scheduled for one more amateur track meet that season, the AAU All-Around Championship. Shortly before the competition, he was hospitalized with an unknown illness—perhaps brought on by too much drinking. Thorpe left the hospital on September 1. On September 2, he won the AAU contest. He took part in all ten events—the 100-yard dash, the 16-pound shot put, the running high jump, the 880-yard walk, the 16-pound hammer throw, the pole vault, the 120-yard high hurdles, the 56-pound weight throw, the running broad jump, and the one-mile run—all held on the same day. "Thorpe is the greatest athlete that ever lived," one former AAU all-around champion told the *New York World*. "He has beaten me fifty ways. Even when I was in my prime I could not do what he did today."

After Thorpe's Olympic victory, a team of medical experts made a study of Thorpe to try to determine why he was such an amazing athlete. They took forty-six measurements of his body and a series of photographs for analysis. They didn't reach any conclusions.

Both amateur and professional athletics wanted Thorpe. The AAU asked him to compete in a series of track meets across the United States. But Thorpe said he was tired and needed a rest. Meanwhile, offers to play professional baseball and other sports flooded in. Show business promoters even asked him to appear onstage, singing, dancing, telling jokes—whatever would bring in audiences.

At first, Thorpe planned to become a professional athlete. But when Warner advised against it, he turned down all the offers. Instead, Warner persuaded Thorpe to return to Carlisle for one last football season. Thorpe also planned to finish his schooling so he could graduate. "It's hard to go back again but it is for my good, so I will make the best of things," Thorpe wrote in a letter to his half brother Frank.

Carlisle's 1912 football squad was even more impressive than the one the year before. The season began with the usual one-sided warm-up games. Carlisle beat Albright College 50–7, Lebanon Valley 45–0, Dickinson 34–0, and Villanova 65–0. The Dickinson game had one showstopping moment: Thorpe was preparing to punt from Carlisle's own end zone. But he missed the snap, which went over his head. Thorpe managed to recover the ball and unexpectedly ran all the way to the other end of the field to score a touchdown.

In the Villanova game, Thorpe played for less than half an hour. But during that time, he scored three touchdowns. By the time the early season was over, the Indians were averaging nearly fifty points a game. Usually Thorpe and his teammates needed nowhere near four downs to advance ten yards—they needed only one.

Carlisle seemed unstoppable, until they met Washington and Jefferson College in Washington, Pennsylvania. Thorpe intercepted the ball four times but could not manage to score a touchdown. And while he attempted three field goals, none of them was good. One was wide, one was short, one was deflected. The game ended in a scoreless tie.

Disheartened, Thorpe and a teammate sneaked off to a bar in Pittsburgh on the journey home. When Pop Warner found out, he was furious. According to one version of the story, Warner had to slam Thorpe's head against the wall to get him to leave the bar. Warner insisted this story was not true. However, Warner did need the help of several other players to drag Thorpe out of the bar and onto the train home.

WARNER'S TRAINING PHILOSOPHY

Pop Warner did not believe in hard training. He thought it was easier to inspire an undertrained athlete than to revive an exhausted one. He had Thorpe and the rest of the football team practice for three hours a day: half an hour of warm-up, half an hour of lecture, and two hours of actual practice. On Sundays, Warner led the team on walks of two or three miles in the countryside. He believed the walks gave players time to think and were good for morale.

The next day, Warner had harsh words for Thorpe. As an Olympic champion, Warner told Thorpe, he had a reputation to uphold. His behavior had hurt not only his own image but also that of the whole team. Warner demanded that Thorpe apologize to his teammates. According to one version of the story, Thorpe not only did that, he also promised never to touch alcohol again.

On October 12, Carlisle played the Syracuse Orangemen, the only team to defeat them during the previous season. In muddy, rainy conditions, the Indians got a slow start. But they rallied in the second half to win the game 33–0. The next week, Carlisle beat the University of Pittsburgh by a score of 45–8. Thorpe scored 32 of Carlisle's 45 points. A *New York Times* headline said it all: "Thorpe Nearly a Team [by himself]."

After defeating Georgetown 34–20, the Indians traveled to Toronto, Canada, for an informal game against a team of Canada's best rugby players. The first half was played by U.S. football rules, the second half by Canadian rugby rules. Under either set of rules, Thorpe and the Indians were the superior team. The final score was 49–1. The next week, Carlisle defeated Lehigh 34–14.

The week after that brought the biggest game of the year—a match against the U.S. Military Academy (called Army) at West Point, New York. Held on November 9, the game was a historic contest between two government-funded schools—one for Native Americans, the other for army officers. Before the game, Warner reminded his team that the fathers and grandfathers of the Army players had killed many Native Americans in the previous century. "If there was one team that the Indians liked to beat more than another," Warner once recalled, "that team was Army."

The Army team was one of the best on the East Coast. Nonetheless, Thorpe and his teammates easily defeated them 27–6. "Thorpe's Indians Crush West Point," read the headline in the *New York Times*. "Standing out resplendent in a galaxy of Indian stars was Jim Thorpe, recently crowned the athletic marvel of the age," the article read. During one run, "Thorpe went through the West Point line as if it were an open door . . . every Cadet [Army player] in the game had his chance, and every one of them failed."

Famously, the Army team included Dwight Eisenhower, who would later become a World War II general and the thirty-fourth U.S. president. According to a legend that even made its way into the *New York Times*, Eisenhower hurt his knee trying to tackle Thorpe and never played football again. However, Eisenhower strongly denied the story. According to Eisenhower, he collided with a teammate while both of them tried to tackle Thorpe. Although they both begged to stay, the coach took them out of the game.

Other myths grew up around the Carlisle-West Point game. According to the most enduring legend, Thorpe ran the length of the field for a touchdown. But the touchdown didn't count because a teammate was called for holding. On the very next play, Thorpe supposedly ran the length of the field again to score another touchdown—and this one was good. The story fit so well with other Thorpe mythology that by the end of his life, even Thorpe believed it was true. In fact, despite his impressive performance, he did not score any of Carlisle's touchdowns in the game.

 At just under six feet, Jim Thorpe was the tallest player on the 1912 Carlisle squad.

The next week brought a matchup with the University of Pennsylvania. At one point, Thorpe ran in an eighty-yard touchdown, which Warner later described as "as beautiful a piece of open-field running as I ever expect to see." During his run, Thorpe was nearly tackled twice, but he managed to shake off his opponent and keep going. But in the second half, Thorpe lost his focus. Thinking the Indians had the game won, Thorpe eased up while the Quakers did not. Carlisle lost, 34–26.

A personal situation might have contributed to Thorpe's poor performance. He had asked Iva Miller, his sweetheart from the year before, to marry him. But she had moved to California, and her relatives there strongly discouraged her from accepting the proposal. Thorpe had also given Miller an engagement ring, but her relatives had taken it away.

Despite his personal troubles, Thorpe concentrated on the final games of the season. The second-to-last game was against the Springfield Training School in Springfield, Massachusetts. Although Springfield put up a tough fight, the Indians won, 30–24, with Thorpe scoring nearly all Carlisle's points.

A few days later, some reporters and curious locals turned out to watch the Indians practice. Among the small crowd was Charles Clancy, who had coached Thorpe as a baseball player in North Carolina. When Clancy noticed Thorpe, he pointed him out to Roy Johnson, a reporter for the *Worcester* (Massachusetts) *Telegram*.

Johnson realized he had accidentally come across a big story. Had Thorpe played minor-league ball in the South? Had he been a professional, not an amateur, when he competed in the Olympic Games? Unbeknownst to Thorpe, Johnson began investigating the rumor.

Carlisle's last game of the season, on Thanksgiving Day, was against Brown University. In the first half, the Indians played badly, although they kept Brown from scoring. Between halves, Warner told his players that it was Thorpe's last game, and they owed it to him to win.

In the second half, Warner recalled, "Brown must have thought a cyclone had blown up, for the Indians swept forward for touchdown after touchdown with resistless fury." In one spectacular play, Thorpe was forced to punt from behind Carlisle's own goal line. He faked the kick and instead ran the ball 110 yards to score a touchdown.

Thorpe's defense was as impressive as his offense. In the second half, Brown came within five yards of scoring a touchdown. Twice, a 192-pound Brown player tried to leap over the Carlisle defensive line. According to the *Providence Journal*, "each time Thorpe caught him in mid-air, and without giving ground an inch, literally hurled him back four yards."

By game's end Thorpe had scored three touchdowns and kicked two field goals for the 32-0 victory. The *Providence Journal* headline told the story: "The real score: Thorpe 32, Brown 0."

Of fourteen games, the 1912 Carlisle Indians had won twelve, lost one, and tied one. They had outscored their opponents 504–114. Of those 504 points, Jim Thorpe had scored 198—an average of 14 points per game. Thorpe was named a first-team All-American halfback for the second year in a row.

When the football season ended, Thorpe returned to Oklahoma for Christmas. He enjoyed not only visiting with his brothers and sisters but also being welcomed back to his hometown as a local hero.

Thorpe returned to Carlisle on January 18, 1913. The following weekend, he attended a dance in the school gym. A graceful dancer, Thorpe won first prize—a chocolate cake—for doing the best two-step in the room. Thorpe, who was known for his generosity, brought the cake back to his dorm to share with the other athletic boys.

Chapter | Eight

Scandal

On January 22, 1913—two months after the rumor first surfaced—the story about Thorpe's alleged professionalism finally broke. "Thorpe with Professional Baseball Team Says Clancy," read the headline in the *Worcester Telegram*.

According to the article, "the great Jim Thorpe, the Sauk and Fox Indian, world's amateur champion athlete, played professional baseball in the Carolina association for two years." The *Worcester Telegram* article also accused Thorpe of public drunkenness and of being cowardly as a ballplayer. The writer speculated, "Whether he will be stripped of his honors and the title of world champion is a question for the athletic authorities to decide."

In the following days, newspapers across the country picked up the story, which grew into the biggest scandal in sports. Thorpe was mostly silent. At one point, as the scandal unfolded, he told the *New York Times* that he did not have any statement. He said only, "I must have time to consider my future plans."

Pop Warner and James Sullivan of the AAU quickly went on the defensive. At first they both denied that Thorpe had played minor-league baseball. But almost immediately, reporters dug up hard evidence that contradicted Warner's and Sullivan's statements. Thorpe had always played under his own name, and sure enough, the records from the Eastern Carolina League included a player named Thorpe. Many eyewitnesses also confirmed the story. Several umpires described Jim Thorpe as one of the most popular players in the league. A Fayetteville teammate described him as "the swiftest man who ever played ball in this section."

Thorpe was in a difficult position. True, he had played summer ball and had received money in exchange. He had actually received much more while playing football at Carlisle, but the payments had come as gifts or in secret. Thorpe was probably confused by the accusations. He had no money, no lawyer, and no adviser except Pop Warner. And he did not understand what professional baseball had to do with amateur track, a completely different sport.

Warner needed to protect himself. If he admitted that he knew Thorpe had played summer baseball, his career as an amateur coach would be over. An investigation might also reveal the questionable finances of the Carlisle Athletic Association—in particular, the fact that Warner essentially paid Carlisle athletes to play.

POP WARNER'S STORY

Jim Thorpe never hid the fact that he had played semiprofessional baseball. According to his official Carlisle record, he had even asked for leave in the summer of 1909 to play baseball in the South. Pop Warner must have known about Thorpe's ball playing, but he never admitted it. Warner claimed that he thought Thorpe had spent the summer of 1909 at home in Oklahoma.

Like Warner, James Sullivan must have known that Thorpe had played summer ball. Thorpe had never played a full baseball season with Carlisle, yet Sullivan had once called Thorpe "a splendid baseball player." Thorpe was the outstanding amateur athlete in the United States. If Sullivan admitted that he knew Thorpe had not upheld the amateur ideal, both Sullivan's career and the future of the AAU would be in doubt.

As the scandal built, Warner and Sullivan made a secret deal. They decided that Thorpe would have to take all the blame. They would continue to lie, saying they knew nothing about Thorpe's semiprofessional career. Warner called in Thorpe for a meeting.

He told Thorpe that the honorable thing to do was to admit his mistake and publicly confess to playing summer baseball.

Warner then wrote a letter of confession addressed to the AAU. Thorpe recopied the letter in his own hand and signed it, as if he had actually written it. "I never realized until now what a big mistake I made by keeping it a secret about my ball playing and I am sorry I did so," the letter read in part. "I hope I would be partly excused because of the fact that I was simply an Indian schoolboy and did not know all about such things." Warner later told the media that "the boys at the Indian school were children mentally and did not understand the fine distinctions between amateurism and professionalism."

On January 27, 1913, five days after the *Worcester Telegram* story appeared, Warner personally took the letter to the AAU in New York. The following day, many newspapers ran Thorpe's letter in full. The AAU decided to banish Thorpe from the amateur ranks and strip him of his Olympic and post-Olympic medals. His trophies would go back to the International Olympic Committee. His records would be erased from the books.

The AAU's swift, brutal decision amazed many of the nation's sportswriters. Like Thorpe, the *Philadelphia Times* wondered what baseball had to do with track. According to a *Times* editorial, "All aspiring athletes will do well to ponder this action of the Amateur Athletic Union and not play croquet, Ping-Pong, tiddly winks, or button-button-who's-got-the-button for compensation. It puts them in the ranks of professionals and absolutely disqualifies them from being able to run, jump, hurdle, throw the discus, pole vault, or wrestle." The *Buffalo Enquirer* pointed out the hypocrisy in the AAU's amateur ideal. It noted that AAU staffers were certainly not expected to work for free.

❝*I played baseball in 1909 and 1910 in the Carolina League but I had no idea I was a pro. I got $60 a month for expenses and that's all. I wouldn't even have tried for the Olympic team had I thought I was a pro. If Warner had backed me up, I wouldn't have had to send back the trophies in the first place.*❞

—JIM THORPE IN 1948, RECALLING THE SCANDAL

Sportswriters and sports fans also noted that, unlike many other college athletes who played summer ball, Thorpe had played under his own name. He had never attempted to be dishonest. But he was the one being punished.

Around the world, editors and sportswriters weighed in on Thorpe's behalf. P. J. Moss wrote in London's *Daily Mirror* that many British Olympians had taken secret payments and gotten away with it. "Unfortunately Thorpe is only one of many," Moss wrote. "He was unlucky enough to be found out, but . . . the fact remains that America had the best man in the Pentathlon and Decathlon events."

The secretary of the Swedish Olympic Committee pointed out that Thorpe was entitled to keep his prizes. According to the rules of the 1912 Olympics, any objections to a competitor's amateur status had to be made within thirty days of the end of the Games. Yet almost six months had passed before the question of Thorpe's status came up.

Nonetheless, the U.S. Olympic Committee, following the AAU's lead, insisted on penalizing Thorpe. Thorpe had to give back his medals and trophies. His gold medals in the pentathlon and decathlon went to the second-place finishers. Thorpe became the first athlete in history to have his name stricken from Olympic records for professionalism.

❝ *I cannot decide whether I was well named or not. Many a time the path has gleamed bright for me, but just as often it has been dark and bitter indeed.* ❞

—JIM THORPE,
REFLECTING ON HIS NATIVE AMERICAN NAME, BRIGHT PATH

Thorpe accepted the U.S. Olympic Committee's decision quietly. Not even his closest friends understood his response. Maybe he was so deeply hurt that he could not express himself.

Or maybe the medals were unnecessary, because he knew he had proven he was the best all-around athlete in the world. When some supporters began to raise money as replacement for his medals and trophies, Thorpe asked them to give the money to charity instead.

Years later, Thorpe remembered that sorry period. "Basically, they used me as a guinea pig to make up the rules," he said. If he had to do it over again, he said, he would not have taken Warner's advice. He would have kept his medals.

Chapter Nine

Baseball and Football

In the wake of the scandal, Jim Thorpe once again received offers to play sports professionally. Football was his best sport and the one he enjoyed the most. But in 1913, professional football in the United States was only getting started. Early professional teams were small, poorly funded, and often went out of business. They were nowhere near as popular as the major college teams.

Baseball, the nation's favorite sport, was a much safer bet. The Chicago White Sox, the Pittsburgh Pirates, the Saint Louis Browns, and the Cincinnati Reds all wanted to sign Thorpe. According to one story, Thorpe was just about to accept Cincinnati's offer when John McGraw, manager of the New York Giants, phoned Pop Warner, who was acting as Thorpe's agent. Warner recalled, "He offered to double the Reds' offer. On hearing this, I told McGraw he had a deal."

But McGraw and the other managers wanted Thorpe for his fame as much as for his playing ability. In fact, McGraw had never met Thorpe before and certainly had never seen him play. Nonetheless, McGraw told the press, "If he doesn't make a ballplayer I miss my guess."

On February 1, 1913—ten days after the *Worcester Telegram* article appeared—Thorpe signed with the New York Giants. According to his yearlong contract, he would earn $6,000, plus a $500 signing bonus. Thorpe had become the highest-paid recruit in baseball and one of the highest-paid untested players ever signed to a professional baseball team. "It has been my ambition to become a big-league ballplayer when my school days were over, and now I have a chance to have the ambition of my life realized," Thorpe said at the signing.

The same day Thorpe signed with the Giants, he officially withdrew from Carlisle. It had been nearly nine years since he had first enrolled. Yet by age twenty-five, he had not managed to earn a diploma from any of the school's programs. According to the final entry in his official school record, dated February 1, 1913, Thorpe was "discharged to play ball."

Despite the generous salary, Thorpe's first season with the Giants was difficult. McGraw did not know how to manage Thorpe to get the best performance out of him. Extremely controlling, McGraw thought his way of doing things was the only way.

Thorpe's sense of humor and independence irritated McGraw. And while Thorpe could run fast and throw hard, his basic baseball skills needed polishing. Rather than helping Thorpe develop his natural ability, McGraw made fun of him for not keeping up with his more experienced teammates. Thorpe spent much of the 1913 season on the bench, hating it the whole time.

At the end of his first season in professional baseball, Thorpe returned to Carlisle to marry Iva Miller, who had finally won the consent of her relatives. The ceremony was held on October 14, 1913, at Saint Patrick's Church. Since both Miller's and Thorpe's parents were dead, Superintendent Friedman gave the bride away and hosted a reception for the couple at his home.

WEDDING NEWS

Even though Iva Miller had very little Native American blood, several press reports described her as a "beautiful Cherokee Indian maiden." Two different companies filmed the couple's wedding and included the scene in newsreels (news footage shown in movie theaters before the main feature).

Afterward, the Thorpes left on an unusual honeymoon—a goodwill baseball tour around the world. On this tour, the

Giants and the Chicago White Sox played exhibition games in sixteen states and fourteen countries, including Japan, China, Australia, Italy, France, and England.

When the newlyweds returned in the spring of 1914, they settled into a New York City apartment near the Giants' ballpark. The following year, their first child, James Francis Thorpe Jr., was born. Thorpe adored his young son.

Soon after James Jr. was born, Thorpe accepted an offer to play professional football, partly to earn more money to support his family. He signed with the Canton Bulldogs of Canton, Ohio, for $250 a game (very good money in those early days). "The deal paid off even beyond my greatest expectations," Bulldogs manager Jack Cusack recalled. "Jim was an attraction as well as a player." When Thorpe played, attendance skyrocketed. Thorpe later became captain of the Bulldogs.

Thorpe made quite an impression on a Bulldogs teammate with his behavior at breakfast. "Jim would blow into the dining room about ten [in the morning, before a game] and immediately be surrounded by waiters," the teammate recalled. "He would always begin by saying he wasn't very hungry. This is what usually followed: grapefruit, cereal, half a dozen eggs with ham, sirloin steak with onions, fried potatoes, sausages, rolls, a pot of coffee."

> 66 *He'd run down the field and in his wake you'd see a string of prostrate [lying down] football players. He seemed to run with his knees up to his chin. . . . He was like an oak tree doing a hundred yards in ten seconds.* 99
>
> —CARP JULIAN, CANTON BULLDOGS TEAMMATE

Information about this period of Thorpe's athletic career is almost nonexistent. The first pro football teams did not keep records or statistics. The teams were filled with college athletes playing under false names. By one account, sports photographers were afraid to take pictures of the games, for fear they would be roughed up afterward by the "amateur" players they had caught on film.

Like college games, early professional football games were brutal. Thorpe, however, was more than able to hold his own. Player George Halas, who later became the head coach of the Chicago Bears, recalled Thorpe's style. "He was a great defensive player. His tackling was as unusual as his running style—he never tackled with his arms and shoulders. He'd leg-whip the ball carrier. If he hit you from behind, he'd throw that big body across your back and . . . near break you in two."

Meanwhile, Thorpe continued to play for the Giants, mostly specializing in warming the bench. "I felt like a sitting hen, not a ballplayer," he once complained. In three seasons, Thorpe appeared in sixty-six games and got just twenty-three hits—not much value for the Giants' money.

Tough Customers

The crowds at early professional football games were just as rough as the players. At the end of the 1915 championship game between the Canton Bulldogs and their archrival, the Massillon Tigers, a referee made a controversial call that was critical to the outcome of the game. Fans got upset and broke down the fences around the playing field, ending the game. Fearing for their safety, officials refused to give a decision on the referee's call right then. Instead, they delivered their decision in a sealed letter to be opened half an hour after midnight, giving them time to get out of town. According to their decision, Canton and Massillon—small Ohio towns about ten miles apart—tied for the so-called world football championship.

After three seasons as an outfielder with the Giants, Thorpe joined the Cincinnati Reds in 1917. Finally, he got the chance to play. By the end of the season, he had batted .247 in seventy-seven games—a respectable if not exceptional average.

Later that year, the Giants needed extra players for their World Series game against the Chicago White Sox. Once again, Thorpe returned to the Giants' bench. He did not return to Cincinnati but instead stayed with New York.

CARLISLE CLOSES

Carlisle Indian Industrial School was closed in 1918, near the end of World War I. The U.S. War Department took over the facility and opened a new hospital there. In 1951 the facility became the U.S. Army War College.

In 1918 Thorpe's personal life took a tragic turn. His son, James, died at the age of three. According to one source, the cause was infantile paralysis. According to another, he was a victim of the 1918 influenza pandemic, which killed an estimated fifty million people worldwide.

For Thorpe, his young son's death was the greatest tragedy of his life, one that made the loss of his Olympic medals seem meaningless in comparison. "He was heartbroken when that boy died," Iva later remarked. "His drinking problem increased after that." Thorpe and Iva had three more children, Gail, Charlotte, and Grace, although biographers do not list their birth dates.

Thorpe played his final season of major-league baseball for the Boston Braves in 1919. His batting average was a strong .327 in sixty games. In the early 1920s, Thorpe also played with minor-league teams, including the Akron Internationals.

As Thorpe's baseball career was winding down, professional football in the United States was becoming better organized. A new league, the American Professional Football Association (APFA, later named the National Football League, or NFL), formed in 1920. The league included eleven teams (four from Ohio, four from Illinois, one from Indiana, and two from New York). Just days after Thorpe finished the baseball season with the Akron Internationals, he became president of the new football league.

Thorpe was mainly a figurehead, or symbolic, president, chosen because at age thirty-three he remained one of the nation's greatest football players. In fact, Thorpe was not particularly gifted at administration or networking. He left the job after just a year. Thorpe preferred playing football to organizing a football league.

❝I hit the jackpot by signing the famous Jim Thorpe, the Sac and Fox Indian from Oklahoma who was rated then . . . as the greatest footballer and all-around athlete that the world of sports has ever seen.❞

—JACK CUSACK, CANTON BULLDOGS MANAGER

After leaving the APFA, he formed his own football team, known as Jim Thorpe's Oorang Indians. As was common with early professional teams, Thorpe's team was named after its sponsor, the Oorang Kennels in La Rue, Ohio. (In exchange for publicity, the company provided money to support the team.) To fill his all-Native American team, Thorpe brought in players from across the United States, including many talented Carlisle alumni.

The Oorang Indians were a cross between a professional football team and a novelty act. Players adopted joke Native American names such as Bear Behind. At halftime, they staged a skit in which Native Americans fought the Germans—U.S. enemies during World War I (1914–1918). The team lost as often as it won, but Thorpe and the players enjoyed themselves. The team disbanded at the end of its second season.

Around this time, Thorpe left his family. He and Iva divorced, although he remained in touch with his three daughters. Two years later, in 1925, Thorpe remarried. His second wife, Freeda Kirkpatrick, was a former office worker for the Oorang Indians. Thorpe was thirty-eight, while Kirkpatrick was just seventeen. The couple eventually had four boys: Carl, William, Richard, and John.

For the last five years of his football career, Thorpe played for the Rock Island Independents, the New York Football Giants, and various other clubs. As he grew older, Thorpe was noticeably slower. But his kicking remained strong and accurate, and his tackling could beat many younger players in their prime. One opponent remembered being tackled by a thirty-nine-year-old Thorpe. He said afterward that he had never been hit harder in his life.

Around this time, Thorpe also played professional basketball. In 2005, a book collector unexpectedly found evidence of Thorpe's basketball career. In an old book purchased at a New York auction, the collector found an unused ticket for a basketball game. The ticket listed a team name, "Jim Thorpe and his world famous Indians," and a date, March 1, 1927, but no city. After some research, the collector discovered that the basketball game had been played in Warren, Pennsylvania. It was part of a forty-five-game tour, mostly played in Pennsylvania towns, in 1927 and 1928. Until the discovery, most of Thorpe's biographers had no idea that he had once played professional basketball. Even Thorpe's son John was surprised.

Although he had hated his years at the Sauk and Fox school and at Haskell, Jim Thorpe sent his own children to Indian boarding schools.

In 1928 Thorpe was playing for the NFL's Chicago Cardinals when he announced his retirement from sports. He was forty-two years old.

Chapter | Ten

All-American

When Jim Thorpe's athletic career ended, he struggled to support himself and his growing family. The Great Depression—an enormous downturn in the worldwide economy that began in 1929—made this job even more difficult. The Thorpes moved to Southern California, where Jim took odd jobs and tried to break into show business as an actor. In 1929 he sold the rights to his life story to the movie studio MGM for $1,500—a tiny sum by Hollywood standards. The film adaptation, *Red Man of Carlisle*, was never made.

Eventually, Thorpe did appear in small roles in Hollywood films. Usually he played Native Americans, occasionally athletes or tough guys. His first role was a bit part in the 1931 film *Battling with Buffalo Bill*.

In 1931 Thorpe appeared with big stars Tom Mix and Mickey Rooney in *My Pal, the King*, a comedy about U.S.

performers stranded in eastern Europe. He also had an uncredited part—meaning his name did not appear on the list of performers—as a dancer in the original *King Kong* in 1933. In the mid-1930s, as Hollywood began to recover from the Great Depression, Thorpe found more work. In 1935 he appeared in seventeen films, almost always uncredited.

In 1932 Jim Thorpe was too poor to afford a ticket to the Summer Olympics in Los Angeles. U.S. vice president Charles Curtis, who was part Native American, invited Thorpe to the opening ceremonies as his guest. The crowd of more than one hundred thousand gave Thorpe a standing ovation.

In the late 1930s, Thorpe became involved in Native American politics. By then, Native Americans were U.S. citizens. Thorpe believed they no longer needed special treatment by the U.S. government. In 1937 Thorpe returned to Oklahoma, where he campaigned for the abolition of the Bureau of Indian Affairs, the U.S. government agency that looked out for the welfare of Native Americans. "The six thousand now employed in political jobs administering Indian affairs should be dismissed and the Indians should begin management of their own business," Thorpe said.

"The Indian should be permitted to shed his inferiority complex and live like a normal American citizen."

Later, Thorpe turned to professional lecturing. He gave up to four lectures a week at schools across the country. In his talks, Thorpe spoke about his career, Native American culture and traditions, the current sports season, and the importance of sports in modern life. For effect, he delivered his lectures dressed in traditional Native clothing.

Thorpe continued to drink heavily. On one occasion, he was fined for drunk driving. Another time, the police took him to jail for being drunk and disorderly. Thorpe would also leave his family for two or three weeks at a time without explaining where he was. To his seven children, Thorpe was a kind and loving father when he was around, but that wasn't very often. Frustrated with her husband's behavior, his second wife, Freeda, filed for divorce. The couple divorced in 1941.

When World War II (1939–1945) began, Thorpe wanted to serve in the military. By then in his early fifties, Thorpe was considered too old for the armed forces. He ended up working as a security guard at a Ford plant in Dearborn, Michigan, in 1942. Although Thorpe appeared to be in good health, he suffered a heart attack in 1943.

After his recovery, Thorpe joined the U.S. Merchant Marine. (A fleet of ships and their crews, the merchant marine transports cargo during peacetime and transports soldiers, weapons, and supplies during wartime.) Thorpe was assigned to the USS *Southwest Victory*, which carried ammunition to troops stationed in India. He served as the ship's carpenter.

Once when Thorpe was out driving with his sons, they got a flat tire but did not have a jack. As Thorpe's son John recalled, he and his brothers loosened the lug nuts. Then Thorpe held up the car while the young men changed the tire.

Thorpe married for a third time in 1945. His new wife, Patricia Askew, was a canny businesswoman who took control of Thorpe's career. Under her management, Thorpe's lecture fee increased to $500, plus expenses.

In 1948 the AAU began organizing a Junior Olympics for teenagers. Thorpe supported the new program as a way to keep teenagers out of trouble. Later that year, Thorpe took a job with the Chicago Park District. In this job, he appeared at parks throughout the city, promoting the Junior Olympics and teaching children the basics of track. The AAU held the first Junior Olympics, limited to competitors under age fifteen, later that year in Cleveland.

Also in 1948, Thorpe helped coach the Israel National Soccer Team for its match against the U.S. Olympic Soccer Team. During halftime, Thorpe gave a kicking demonstration. Even at sixty years old, he could still punt a ball eventy-five yards.

---

66 *He was so easygoing, so trusting. He was always concerned about people in distress. One of his friends needed $105 to pay his wife's hospital bill. Jim gave him the $100 he had and borrowed the extra $5. I discovered after that the friend didn't even have a wife. I guess you could say Jim had two-way pockets. . . . You wouldn't think a man could be so perfect. He didn't have a mean bone in his body.* 99

—PATRICIA ASKEW THORPE, JIM'S THIRD WIFE

In 1950 an Associated Press poll named Jim Thorpe the greatest football player of the half century. A few weeks later, another Associated Press survey of sportswriters named him the greatest male athlete of the half century. Of the nearly four hundred sportswriters and radio commentators who had participated in the poll, 252 had chosen Thorpe. Baseball player Babe Ruth, with eighty-six votes, had come in a distant second. In 1951 Thorpe was inducted into the College Football Hall of Fame.

Although the parts were small, Jim Thorpe worked steadily in the movies until 1950. That year, he appeared in his final film, playing a member of the Navajo tribe in *Wagon Master*.

Also in 1951, Hollywood released *Jim Thorpe—All American*, a film about Thorpe's life. The movie starred Burt Lancaster as Thorpe, along with a nearly all-white cast. (Lancaster later won an Academy Award for his role in the move *Elmer Gantry*.) A fictionalized biography, the film took major liberties with Thorpe's life story.

In the film, Thorpe has no twin brother, and his father is portrayed as a gentle man who refuses to whip his son. Thorpe decides to go out for the football team to impress a girl he likes. And Pop Warner is portrayed as Thorpe's biggest defender during the Olympic scandal.

Thorpe participated in the making of the film as an adviser. He was paid $15,000, the only money he received from the film. Despite his involvement, *Jim Thorpe—All American* contained many inaccuracies about Native American culture. Nonetheless, the film did well at the box office and received mostly positive reviews.

> **❝**Some ridiculous stories have been published in magazines and books and have been solemnly repeated by reliable writers. . . . More lies have been written about Jim Thorpe than about any player in football history.**❞**
>
> —ALEXANDER M. WEYAND, FOOTBALL HISTORIAN

In 1952 Thorpe had surgery to remove a cancerous growth from his lip. Later that year, he had another heart attack. On March 28, 1953, Thorpe suffered a third heart attack while he and his wife were eating dinner. He died later that day at the age of sixty-five. He was buried in Shawnee, Oklahoma, near his birthplace.

Glory Restored

After Jim Thorpe's death, his widow, Patricia, hoped to persuade the state of Oklahoma to build a monument to him. When her efforts failed, she traveled to Carlisle, Pennsylvania, to meet with town officials and later to Philadelphia to meet with the NFL commissioner.

During her trip, Patricia heard about two small Pennsylvania towns, Mauch Chunk and East Mauch Chunk. The two neighboring towns had established a fund to attract industry to the area. They were thinking about changing their names. Patricia contacted the towns' officials and proposed that the two towns merge into a new town called Jim Thorpe. The towns' citizens agreed. Patricia had Thorpe's body moved from Oklahoma and reburied in Jim Thorpe, Pennsylvania, in 1954.

"This provoked a great deal of publicity," the editor of the local newspaper recalled, "and as time went on this town got more coverage over this Jim Thorpe story than anything that had ever happened at any time in the past." As well as a memorial to Thorpe, officials in the new town planned a Jim Thorpe sports complex, a cancer research center, a museum, and a motel. But nothing beyond the memorial was ever built.

In 1955 the National Football League named its Most Valuable Player award the Jim Thorpe Trophy. In 1963 Thorpe entered the Pro Football Hall of Fame.

Meanwhile, friends and family—especially daughters Charlotte and Grace—waged a long campaign to have Jim Thorpe's Olympic medals restored. Grace recalled that her father never tried to do this himself and never complained that his medals had been taken away. "He was very philosophical about it, he wasn't bitter at all," she commented.

In the 1970s, while doing research for the biography *Jim Thorpe: World's Greatest Athlete*, historian Robert Wheeler tracked down a copy of the rule book for the 1912 Olympics. He realized that, according to the rules, the charges against Thorpe had been made five months too late. Armed with this information, Wheeler collected 250,000 signatures on a petition to the IOC. The petition stated that Thorpe's medals had been wrongly taken.

In 1973 the AAU finally restored Thorpe's amateur status. But the IOC would not budge on restoring his medals.

Meanwhile, honors for Thorpe continued to roll in. In 1975 he entered the National Track and Field Hall of Fame. In a 1977 national poll, *Sport* magazine named Thorpe the greatest American football player in history.

In 1982, finally succumbing to public pressure, the IOC passed a resolution restoring Thorpe's honors. On January 13, 1983, the IOC president presented duplicates of Thorpe's gold medals to two of his children. In 1997 the AAU gave the Thorpe family the medals he had won for his post-Olympic all-around victory. According to an AAU official, "[Restoring the medals] was the last thing the AAU had to do to make things right for Jim Thorpe."

In a 2000 Internet poll, ESPN and ABC named Jim Thorpe the greatest athlete of the century. Indeed, Thorpe was one of the most talented and versatile athletes in modern sports. He remains the only U.S. athlete to excel at the amateur and professional level in so many different sports—track and field, football, baseball, and basketball. With the reinstatement of his Olympic medals, he can be remembered as he always should have been: as the greatest all-around athlete of the twentieth century.

PERSONAL STATISTICS

Name:

James Francis Thorpe

Native American Name:

Wa-Tho-Huck (Bright Path)

Born:

May 22, 1887

Died:

March 28, 1953

Height:

5' 11"

Weight:

185 lbs.

SELECTED CAREER STATISTICS

Record with Carlisle Indians Football Team

1907	10 wins, 1 loss
1908	10 wins, 2 losses, 1 tie
1911	11 wins, 1 loss
1912	12 wins, 1 loss, 1 tie

1912 Olympic Games, Stockholm, Sweden
Pentathlon (gold medal)

Long jump	23 feet 2.7 inches	first place
Javelin throw	153 feet 2.95 inches	second place
200-meter race	22.9 seconds	first place
Discus throw	116 feet 8.4 inches	first place
1,500-meter race	4 minutes 44.8 seconds	first place

Decathlon (gold medal)

100-meter race	11.2 seconds	second place
Long jump	22 feet 2.3 inches	second place
Shot put	42 feet 5.45 inches	second place
High jump	6 feet 1.6 inches	first place
400-meter race	47.6 seconds	second place
110-meter high hurdles	15.6 seconds	first place
Discus throw	121 feet 3.9 inches	second place
Pole vault	10 feet 7.95 inches	third place
Javelin throw	149 feet 11.2 inches	fourth place
1,500-meter race	4 minutes 40.1 seconds	first place

Major-League Baseball Batting Average

New York Giants	1913	.143
New York Giants	1914	.194
New York Giants	1915	.231
Cincinnati Reds	1917	.247
New York Giants	1917	.193
New York Giants	1918	.248
New York Giants	1919	.333
Boston Braves	1919	.327

Professional Football Games Played

Canton Bulldogs	1920	9 games
Cleveland Indians	1921	5 games
Oorang Indians	1922	5 games
Oorang Indians	1923	9 games
Rock Island Independents	1924	9 games
New York Football Giants/ Rock Island Independents	1925	5 games
Canton Bulldogs	1926	9 games
Chicago Cardinals	1928	1 games

SOURCES

1   Robert W. Wheeler, *Jim Thorpe: World's Greatest Athlete* (Norman: University of Oklahoma Press, 1979), 54.

2   Ibid., 54.

2   Ibid., 55.

2   Ibid.

3   Bill Crawford, *All American: The Rise and Fall of Jim Thorpe* (Hoboken, NJ: Wiley, 2005), 9.

8   Ibid., 14.

8   Wheeler, *Jim Thorpe*, 9.

10   Crawford, *All American*, 20.

10   Ibid., 17.

11   Crawford, *All American*, 49.

12   Jack Newcombe, *The Best of the Athletic Boys: The White Man's Impact on Jim Thorpe* (New York: Doubleday, 1975), 11.

14   Wheeler, *Jim Thorpe*, 10.

14   Ibid., 12.

17   Crawford, *All American*, 51.

18   Newcombe, *Best of the Athletic Boys*, 62.

23   Wheeler, *Jim Thorpe*, 50.

24–25   Ibid., 52.

30   Crawford, *All American*, 79.

31   Ibid., 83.

31   Ibid., 92.

31   Wheeler, *Jim Thorpe*, 67.

33   Crawford, *All American*, 109.

33   Wheeler, *Jim Thorpe*, 67.

33   Ibid.

33   Ibid.

36   Ibid., 64.

36   Crawford, *All American*, 93.

38   Ibid., 123.

38   Wheeler, *Jim Thorpe*, 78.

40   Crawford, *All American*, 125.

43   Ibid., 134.

45   Wheeler, *Jim Thorpe*, 73.

45   Crawford, *All American*, 138.

47   Wheeler, *Jim Thorpe*, 92.

49   "Carlisle Man Has Matters His Own Way in Tryout Contest," *New York Times*, May 19, 1912, C8.

49   Crawford, *All American*, 165.

51   Newcombe, Best of the Athletic Boys, 182.

52   Crawford, *All American*, 167.

55   Newcombe, *Best of the Athletic Boys*, 185.

55   Crawford, *All American*, 173.

57–58   Wheeler, *Jim Thorpe*, 109.

59   Newcombe, *Best of the Athletic Boys*, 186.

61   Crawford, *All American*, 180.

61   Newcombe, *Best of the Athletic Boys*, 188.

62   Wheeler, *Jim Thorpe*, 118.

63   Newcombe, *Best of the Athletic Boys*, 193.

65   "Thorpe Nearly a Team: Famous Indian Great Star in Indians' Victory at Pittsburgh," *New York Times*, October 19, 1912, S1.

66   Crawford, *All American*, 188.

66   "Thorpe's Indians Crush West Point," *New York Times*, November 10, 1912, S1.

67   Crawford, *All American*, 192.

69   Ibid., 193.

69   Newcombe, *Best of the Athletic Boys*, 207.

69   Ibid.

71   Crawford, *All American*, 198.

72   "Thorpe Has Nothing to Say," *New York Times*, January 28, 1913, 3.

72   Crawford, *All American*, 201.

73   Newcombe, *Best of the Athletic Boys*, 152.

74   "Olympic Prizes Lost; Thorpe No Amateur; Carlisle Indian Admits He Once Played Professional Baseball in the South," *New York Times*, January 28, 1913, 1.

74   Crawford, *All American*, 205.

74–75   Newcombe, *Best of the Athletic Boys*, 148.

75   Wheeler, *Jim Thorpe*, 212.

75–76   "British Sympathy for 'Jim' Thorpe, *New York Times*, January 30, 1913, 4.

76   Wheeler, *Jim Thorpe*, 201.

77   Crawford, *All American*, 210.

78   Ibid., 211.

79   "Thorpe Is to Play Ball with Giants," *New York Times*, February 1, 1913, 1.

79 "Thorpe Signs Giant Contact for a
    Year," *New York Times*, February 2,
    1913, S1.

79 Newcombe, *Best of the Athletic
    Boys*, 211.

80 "James Thorpe to Marry Indian
    Girl," *New York Times*, September 2,
    1913, 9.

81 Wheeler, *Jim Thorpe*, 169.

81 Newcombe, *Best of the Athletic
    Boys*, 226.

82 Wheeler, *Jim Thorpe*, 187.

82 Crawford, *All American*, 226.

82–83 Newcombe, *Best of the Athletic
    Boys*, 215.

84 Ibid., 232.

85 Wheeler, *Jim Thorpe*, 169.

89–90 Ibid., 196.

92 Ibid., 226.

94 Ibid., 2.

95–96 Ibid., 230.

96 Dave Anderson, "Jim Thorpe's
    Medals," *New York Times*, June 22,
    1975, 199.

97 Crawford, *All American*, 226.

BIBLIOGRAPHY

Crawford, Bill. *All American: The Rise and Fall of Jim Thorpe.* Hoboken, NJ: Wiley, 2005.

Curtiz, Michael, director. *Jim Thorpe—All American*, VHS. Burbank, CA: Warner Home Video, 1992.

Newcombe, Jack. *The Best of the Athletic Boys: The White Man's Impact on Jim Thorpe.* Garden City, NY: Doubleday, 1975.

Wheeler, Robert W. *Jim Thorpe: World's Greatest Athlete.* Norman: University of Oklahoma Press, 1979.

WEBSITES

Jim Thorpe Association

http://www.jimthorpeassoc.org

Established in 1986, the Jim Thorpe Association encourages excellence in sports, health, and fitness.

College Football Hall of Fame

http://www.collegefootball.org/famersearch.php?id=10005

Jim Thorpe's early fame came during his college football career with Carlisle. This website offers a brief profile on Thorpe and his college achievements.

Pro Football Hall of Fame

http://www.profootballhof.com/hof/member.jsp?player_id=213

Jim Thorpe entered the Pro Football Hall of Fame in 1963. This Web page provides a biography and brief details on Thorpe's pro football career.

USA Track and Field Hall of Fame

http://www.usatf.org/HallOfFame/TF/showsBio.asp?HOFIDS=170

This Web page is dedicated to Jim Thorpe, inducted into the National Track and Field Hall of Fame in 1975.

INDEX

A
Akron Internationals, 85
Albright College, 32, 63
All-American, 34, 48, 69
Amateur Athletic Union
    (AAU), 27, 43, 55, 72-
    76, 91-92, 96-97
Amateur Athletic Union All-
    Around Championship,
    61-62
American Professional
    Football Association
    (APFA), 85-86
Anadarko Champions, 42
Archiquette, Chauncey, 13
Army, 65-67
Askew, Patricia. *See*
    Thorpe, Patricia Askew
Atlanta Braves, 24

B
Battling With Buffalo Bill, 88
Big Ten Conference, 31
Blackhawks, 24
Boston Athletic Association,
    49
Boston Braves, 84
Brown University, 40, 47,
    68-69
Bucknell University, 30
Bureau of Indian Affairs, 89

C
Camp, Walter, 34, 48
Canton Bulldogs, 81-83, 85
Carlisle Indian Industrial
    School, 1-3, 16-37, 40-
    51, 60-70, 72, 79, 84,
    86
Carlisle Indian Industrial
    School Athletic
    Association, 30, 73
Chicago Bears, 82
Chicago Cardinals, 87
Chicago Park District, 92
Chicago White Sox, 78, 81,
    84
Cincinnati Reds, 78, 83-84
Clancy, Charles, 68, 71
College Football Hall of
    Fame, 93

cricket, 11
Cusack, Jack, 81, 85
Czar Nicholas II, 58

D
decathlon, 49-50, 55-59, 76
de Coubertin, Baron Pierre,
    50, 54
Dickinson College, 32, 44,
    63

E
Eastern Carolina League,
    37, 39-40, 72, 75
Eisenhower, Dwight D., 38,
    66
Exendine, Albert, 26-28, 31,
    42-43

F
Fayetteville Highlanders, 42
Friedman, Moses, 41, 43,
    51, 61, 80

G
Garden Grove, 15-16
Georgetown, 45, 65
Great Depression, 88-89
Gustav V, 58-59

H
Halas, George, 82
Harvard, 31, 34, 46-47
Haskell Institute, 12-14, 16,
    19, 90

I
Indian Territory, 4-8, 16-17
International Olympic
    Committee, 74, 96-97
Israeli National Soccer
    Team, 92

J
Jim Thorpe: All-American, 93
Jim Thorpe, Pennsylvania,
    96
Jim Thorpe's Oorang
    Indians, 86
Jim Thorpe Trophy, 96

*Jim Thorpe: World's Greatest
    Athlete*, 96
Johnson, Roy, 68
Junior Olympics, 91-92

K
King Kong, 89
Kirkpatrick, Freeda. *See*
    Thorpe, Freeda
    Kirkpatrick

L
lacrosse, 12, 41
Lafayette College, 45. 50
Lancaster, Burt, 93
Lebanon Valley College, 44,
    63
Libby, Joe, 37-38

M
McGraw, John, 78-80
Miller, Iva. *See* Thorpe, Iva
    Miller
Moore, Marianne, 48
Mount Pleasant, Frank, 31-
    32
Mount Saint Mary's College,
    44
My Pal, My King, 88

N
National Collegiate Athletic
    Association (NCAA),
    27-28, 43
National Football League.
    See American
    Professional Football
    Association
National League of
    Professional Base Ball
    Clubs, 36
National Track and Field
    Hall of Fame, 97
Native American politics, 7,
    9, 89
    mascots, 24
New York Giants (football),
    78-84, 86
New York Times, 49, 65-66,
    72

O

Olympics, 32, 49-62, 64, 84, 89, 93, 96
Olympic scandal, 68, 71-77, 93, 96

P

Pennsylvania State College, 26, 33, 40
pentathlon, 49-50, 55, 58, 76
Pittsburgh Athletic Club Indoor Meet, 49
Pittsburgh Pirates, 78
Potawatomi, 5, 7
Pratt, Richard Henry, 17-18
Professional Football Hall of Fame, 96

R

Red Man of Carlisle, 88
Rock Island Independents, 86
Rocky Mount Railroaders, 37-43
Rooney, Mickey, 88
rugby, 65
Ruth, Babe, 93

S

Sauk and Fox School, 9-12, 90
Sauk and Fox tribe, 5-10, 12, 16-18, 51, 71, 85
semiprofessional baseball, 37-43, 72-75
shinny (sport), 12
S.S. *Finland*, 53-54
St. Louis Browns, 78
Stagg, Amos Alonzo, 35
Sullivan, James, 55, 72-73
Swedish Olympic Committee, 76
Syracuse Orangemen, 29, 34, 47, 65

T

Taft, William Howard, 61
Tewanima, Louis, 31-32, 49, 51, 53, 60-61
Thorpe, Carl, 86
Thorpe, Charles "Charlie," 4, 6, 8-11

Thorpe, Charlotte, 84, 96
Thorpe, Charlotte Vieux, 4-8, 10-11, 14
Thorpe Day, 60-61
Thorpe, Frank, 63
Thorpe, Freeda Kirkpatrick, 86, 90
Thorpe, Gail, 84
Thorpe, George, 9, 14
Thorpe, Grace, 84, 96
Thorpe, Hiram, 5-15, 17, 20, 25
Thorpe, Iva Miller, 46, 48, 67-68, 80, 84, 86
Thorpe, James Francis
  acting, 88-89, 93
  baseball, 3, 10-11, 25-26, 32, 36, 62, 68, 78
  basketball, 35, 48, 87
  career statitics, 99
  Carlisle Indian Industrial School, 1-3, 16-37, 40-51, 60-70, 72, 79, 84, 86
  childhood, 4-8
  death, 94
  football, 1-2, 12-14, 25, 27-35, 40-48, 56, 64, 66-69, 72, 78, 81, 85
  Haskell Institute, 12-14, 16, 19, 90
  Olympics, 32, 49-62, 64, 84, 89, 93, 96
  Olympic scandal, 68, 71-77, 93, 96
  personal statistics, 98
  Rocky Mount Railroaders, 37-43
  Sauk and Fox School, 9-12, 90
Thorpe, James Francis Jr., 81, 84
Thorpe, John, 86-87, 91
Thorpe, Julia Mixon, 14
Thorpe, Margaret, 6
Thorpe, Mary, 6, 40
Thorpe, Patricia Askew, 91-92, 95
Thorpe, Richard, 86
Thorpe, William, 86

track and field, 1, 3, 25-26, 31-32, 35-36, 41, 48-50, 55-56, 62, 72, 92

U

United States Merchant Marines, 91
United States Military Academy, 65-67
United States Olympic Committee, 51, 76
United States Olympic Soccer Team, 92
University of Chicago, 31, 35
University of Pennsylvania, 30-31, 34, 45-46, 67
University of Pittsburgh, 40, 45, 65

V

Villanova College, 33, 63

W

Wagon Master, 93
Warner, Glenn Scobey "Pop," 2-3, 19-21, 24-33, 35-36, 40-41, 43, 46-47, 49, 51-53, 60-66, 68-69, 72-75, 77-78, 93
Washington, George, 14
Washington and Jefferson College, 63
Wa-Tho-Huck, 4, 76
West Point. *See* United States Military Academy
Weyand, Alexander M., 94
Wheeler, Robert, 96
White, Walter, 16
Whitney, Caspar, 34
Wieslander, Hugo, 57
Worcester Telegram, 68, 71, 74, 79
World Series, 84
World War I, 84, 86
World War II, 90

Y

Yale, 34, 46
Youngdeer, Jesse, 37